THROUGH THE
RANK

MARIE FORD

ISBN: 979-8-89031-785-8 (sc)
ISBN: 979-8-89031-786-5 (hc)
ISBN: 979-8-89031-787-2 (e)

Because of the dynamic nature of the Internet, any web addresses or links contained in this book may have changed since publication and may no longer be valid. The views expressed in this work are solely those of the author and do not necessarily reflect the views of the publisher, and the publisher hereby disclaims any responsibility for them.

THE EWINGS
PUBLISHING

One Galleria Blvd., Suite 1900, Metairie, LA 70001
(504) 702-6708

This is something I have wanted to do for a long time and promised this would be something I would do to help the public understand what it is like being a department of corrections employee for a corrections officer up to a Correctional Captain were I am presently/Retired.

NOVEMBER 1988

A tornado struck in Raleigh and I remember being scared to come down here after that. I was being told don't go down Glenwood avenue because the tornado came through their and hit K-Mart then and there was debris up and down Glenwood avenue. It struck during earlier morning hours and apartment were struck people were scared caused they had no idea what happen they were sleep and woke up to devastation and confusion, it was terrible.

DECEMBER 1, 1988

I began my employment at North Carolina Correctional Institute for Women, I must add that I have met some very interesting people along the way.

Some type of Law enforcement is something I always wanted to be a part of. I began with submitting an application and was trying to go to Central Prison but I was told I probably would be better at women Prison. I had just about given up hope when they called me and ask me to come for an interview. I was so excited! My Mom and my cousin loaded up and headed to Raleigh.

I will never forget one of the questions ask of me was if an inmate curse me out what would I do? I state I know what I would want to do but I would try and do the right thing and notify my supervisor. Believe it or not that is the only question I could remember. You know before you have your interview you have to fill out all these papers and one was the shift you requested to work. I don't know why they make you fill that out because it didn't matter because all the new people always started 3rd shift and work their way up to the requested shift. It didn't matter who you were or who you knew. 3rd shift was a good starting point because you had the contact needed to determine if you were going to make it or not. I remember having to get a physical there at the prison in the same infirmary that the inmates were in. I don't know if that was supposed to happen or not, I was just glad to get the job at that point it didn't matter to me much. The infirmary/Mental Health was old and run down. It had plywood up where I think at that time they were in the middle of new construction of a new infirmary/Mental Health building. I remember when I along with other new staff went on tour of the facility it felt like you were like paraded to the inmates and they were sizing you up to see that would potentially make it the first day or quit. Well that won't getting ready to happen not with me. I would run with the best of them. I remember the first time I put that uniform on I was so proud of it, you couldn't tell me anything. I always made sure I took pride in my uniform and acted accordingly while wearing it.

I stayed with my best friend in Durham for about a year, traveling back and forth to Raleigh until I found somewhere to stay in Raleigh. I stayed with this elderly couple on Branch Street. I was sleeping in their attic which was not very big. I was telling some of my co-workers I was going to see about getting in the apartments a block away from there and they told me oh no you not either that is a bad area which was Bragg St, well I didn't know I was glad someone told me. I was driving my Moms car back then a deep blue Buick Lesabre and every time I came out to go to work, someone was bending the radio antenna all the way down to the ground. I could not catch who was doing it though. This house since then has been torn down. I don't know what happen to the Lady and man that stayed there. Well I finally rented an apartment off of Avent Ferry Rd. Crab Orchard. I purchased me a little old white Mitsubishi pickup truck and that's what I drove for quite some time. I was so excited about the new job and trying to get things together, it wasn't until later when I sit down and started thinking, which I had a lot of time to do. I said to myself fool you have left home, it got scary for a minute but I pulled out of it. I got to meet and know a lot of people from other facilities. I can't remember how but I met up with some guys from another facility and they ask me was I interested in playing coed softball, of course that was right down my ally. I had been playing since I was 13 years old and taught by the best (RIP). I think I surprised the guys because they didn't know I could really play, I was not just a female to have on the team. I loved every minute of it and looked forwarded to it every year after that. I later moved to Lake Wheeler road where I had retrieve my car 1976 gold tone Ford Elite with a 351 Cleveland motor which use to be used as a drivers educational car. One holiday I went home and I was returning on that Sunday I had all my belongings packed, uniforms pressed and neatly hung on the hook in the back. As I was coming down 86 near South Elementary School (now) I met the MAN! SHP I probably was running about 80 mph in a 45. When he passed me, I saw him put that hat on and he made a U–turn and came behind me, which I had slowed down by then and pulled over and waited for him because I know he got me. So He asks me where I was going in such a hurry. I told him I was trying to get to Raleigh. He looked back in the back seat and saw all that shit I had and the uniforms is what saved me. He told me to slow it down some and let me go. The BIG MAN has always watched out for me and blessed me every day, if it had not been for him I would not be where I am today. God is good all the time, all the time God is good!!!!!

So with the extra time that I had on my hands, I started a hobby of collecting sports cards Basketball, Baseball, Football and Olympics complete sets. All the cards I collected were in 1990s so they are about 25 years old. I stopped collecting about 1995 or 96. I really didn't know what I had until one day I was showing them to a family member. Some of the athletes have gone on to glory, some retired, some still playing. The family member I had shown this to brought me a trading card book with the individual sleeves to place the cards in so they would not be damaged. I was keeping them in shoe boxes. When I lost that urge to collect I removed all the cards from the shoe boxes and place them in 4 card books. That I still have in my possession. I also begin collecting newspaper clippings of Crimes that where committed by the females I was supervising.

Uniforms then were mailman uniforms with a jacket. I train 2 day with a senior staff I remember my first strip search in old roach infested dorm C. I felt so a shame, that was the most degrading thing to me I almost cried. It did not bother the ofc training me. Well I soon got over that after having to do so many searches in Dorm C, I told my Mom I was tired of looking at Ass, tits and pussy. The next working day they threw me in dorm B1 by myself with about 100 inmates. They were in dormitory style setting you had about 50 inmates on both sides with gates that could be secured and you were in the middle at a desk with a radio, flashlight and a telephone. Then inmates were allowed to stay up all night weekends and the holidays. If you go to make rounds you may come back or not, you were the only one in there. So When I arrived at B1 for night duty 10pm - 6am. I relieved second shift staff and they passed over all information and they kind of sniggled and ask you working in here by yourself? I stated yes. They stated well you have a good night. I closed the door and locked it and ALL those inmates ran to the door yelling open the door. I turned around and very loudly stated "let's get something straight right now, I ain't the one, you can come out here and act like you got some sense or stay behind that gate! Well the staff I relieved that night told me the next night when I was put back in B1 that she was standing at the door and you handled your business, I like you. I went to Basic training in February 1989, it was fun back then.

I had only work at NCCIW for about 2 months the next time I was placed in B1 or B2 I was summoned to the Captain, Lieutenants office which then was a little white house with a front section and a back section very little room. When I arrived all the white shirts and a few Sgts were gathered around, I was like Oh Hell what have I done. Well after the sgt just acted like it was so terrible they just couldn't ask me, the Lt stated we received a complaint from B1 or B2 that you were feeling on an inmate's breast. I damn near stopped breathing and stood there in disbelief. Once I gained my composure, I was mad as hell that they lied and then my Supervisors believed what the inmates told them. I stated I came here to work, not play games with offenders and be their friends. Whoever made the complaint LIED! I didn't appreciate the fact that they believed it. I stated I came here to work and do my job. I can also leave here and go somewhere else for a job. Of course it was explain that the complaint was made so it had to be investigated. After I was dismissed I was on my way to the gatehouse because I was going to quit and not look back. Well an officer stopped me before I got to the gatehouse and told me to go to A2 where the Officer there needed me to come help her with something. When I arrive in the building and the officer open the gate I walked in and she closed the gate behind me and would not let me out. Telling me I need to sit down and cool off, I talked with her and told her what happened she stated well you are going to have things happen like that because you are trying to do your job don't just walk out. Well by then most of the staff was aware of what had happen and could not believe it. By this time I had calmed down and returned to work.

After this above incident I began my documentation of everything and everybody because this was a place that things would happen and a month or two later you would get questioned about what happen on this day who was involved, I refused to be caught off guard sitting and scratching my head trying to figure out what happen. So I carried my note pad everywhere. When I was asked what happen on any given day, hold on let me get my book I can tell you. I documented everything from all the staff post assignments, times, dates, what was said to me, what I said to other people. So when the staff found out that I was keeping documentation they would come to me and ask you write me in your little book. I was so particular the Capts and Lts would come to me and ask me what happen on certain dates and time. I even had the Capt to come to me and ask me about an incident that took place and they stated to me, where is your little book because I know you have it written in there and it was.

AUGUST 7, 1989

My first part-time job was at Mission Valley Inn across from NCSU. I worked in Banquets catering. I was working 3rd shift at the time so it worked out great. 1990 was the year that my Grandmother died my

Moms Mother. I was working at Mission Valley Inn when I got that call. I immediately called the Prison and spoke to a supervisor and told them my grandmother had just passed and I would not be in to work. I was told by the Sergeant to hold on let me see if we got enough staff tonight. I was so blown away with their response; I just hung up the phone, furious!!! Later I was told that it was announced in line-up about my loss and the Supervisor made the comment to the effect of well even though we know no one will be able to go they would collect money. They did send a flower. I promised myself if I ever became a Supervisor I would not treat my staff or people that way. I would treat people the way I would want to be treated. However one staff did show up to go to the wake the night before, which later on she proved to be one of my enemies.

During this time we worked as a team and did the job escorts, packing property, picking up property for inmates to transfer the next day. We even had someone to come around and give us breaks once a night. I was working dorm G which is now Dorm D, I had ladies fussing over the telephone in the lobby area one was on the phone and the other one signed the phone log and went back to her room. Once the offender ended her call another offender signed the log and proceeded to use the phone. The other offender came from her room and of course was fussing because someone jumps her. I informed them you don't sign the log if you are not going to use the phone right then. (Now they pre sign for everything or call next.) I had some Ladies at the table playing cards I was standing in the doorway of the dayroom area and observed them passing money. I told them I was giving them fair warning that I did not need to see them passing any more money at the table gambling. They later got up from the table 2 ladies went to bed and the other two were still in the dayroom area.

Sitting there one morning waiting to for relief and the Officer working with me, started laughing at me, they said I was writing a dairy, she was going to burn it because her name was being strood everywhere.

On August 29 1989 in Dorm H during Line-up there was a disturbance. The Sergeant went to investigate and returned stating there was a code 1000 (fight). Another Sgt went out and I followed behind them running to the quad. The 2nd shift Officer opened the gate. I proceeded to help break up the disturbance the inmate was swinging a yellow blow dryer, when I placed my hands on her to keep her from continuously swinging the blow dryer. I proceeded to remove her from the quad with the aid of another staff. Dorm H was reception- New Admissions dorm so you could become faced with any situation at any given time. These inmates were brought in from the county jails from all over the state of North Carolina they may come in ok or fighting, withdrawing, sickly, pregnant. Inmates would get in a verbal argument I would tell them ladies it's too hot to go to dorm C.(Lock up)

Dorm H was just recently built and this was where we would have our Line ups and I was coming out one night going to my assigned post and I see my classmate. I called her name out and she said yeah it's me. I almost didn't recognize her because she was pregnant. It was good to see her at least I knew I was not there all by myself. Her Baby it now a handsome young man.

I made it my business to be very observant and nosey and listened very closely, sometimes I would hear the same things over and then sometimes it was my first time ever hearing what was being spoken, I made it a part of my JOB. There were several Supervisors that I looked up to and gave the upmost respect. I watched them and how they carried themselves and got respect from the staff and inmates. These supervisors were such a big influence in my career and they have no idea. There was the Captain I love to see her walk; it was like she had a pimp. LOL!! When she came through it was like E.F Hutton. Everyone just kind of froze in their tracks. There was a Lieutenant she was just straight forward and bout it bout it she was one that would roll up on you quick you wouldn't know what happen. Then there was a sergeant she was the most influence supervisor cause to me what ever came out her mouth was the bible. I learned immensely from her. Now she was the type of individual she would say what she had to say and if you didn't get it then be ready for what would follow. Then I started to incorporate what I observed into my daily performance. You treat people the way you would want to be treated. All people cannot be treated the same because we all have different mindsets. What may work for one may not work for the other that's for staff and inmates. I continued to observe and other staff and see how they did or didn't do things. My learning has continued throughout my entire career. You never stop learning and you never knew everything because things always changed. I had pretty much set my goals where I want to go and how far. As everyone would always say you ain't gone have no problems with the inmates, it's the staff that's the problem. Now they hit the nail on the head every time. Being jealous and talking about you and anybody else. All in all if I had let those things bother me I would not have made it. The very ones that did all the talking either quit or couldn't make it for whatever reason. I was young and ready to go get it and I did because I got the ultimate ending RETIREMENT!!!!! It is a wonderful feeling; sometimes I forget I'm retired.

Making rounds in the old dorm C you come around those corners and you might see anything. Offenders may be in bed having sex with someone or themselves. You may see someone you know. If that happen you would have to report it up the chain of command and submit documentation. I was in the unit infirmary one night escorting some inmates, when I saw this new admissions sitting there waiting to be seen. I looked at her and they looked at me and I said I know you from somewhere. Oh she didn't like that and stated oh no! You don't know me. I'm almost sure she was from my home town Yanceyville.

I was assigned to Tower - 1/ Gatehouse (now) Security Supervisors was assigned a Vehicle and staff asks for a different vehicle. I inform them that the vehicle they requested was out. The staff left and then returned as I was changing shifts, went in the key box. I told them to get out of the key box! They knew better than going in that key box, stating the car issued had a dent in the bumper. I told them I did not care; don't go back in that key box again.

I was at tower-1 checking IDs and Officer came through, I ask her for her ID and she stated to me you haven't made Sgt yet. I told them that don't have anything to do with it. You need to show me you're ID. I stated to the supervisor the Phoenix Unit staff thinks they are special or something. So later I was in the control center getting my things ready to go home and Officer turns to the Sgt and tells them to tell me to go check IDs. I bit my tongue and did not say anything I got my mess and came out the office. I called the supervisor and told them somebody better talk to that Officer, because she has lost her chances with me. The next time I'm going to blow her out.

I was sitting taking my break eating when the phone rang, I was told I needed to get a wheelchair and come to dorm E right away. To the infirmary retrieved wheelchair, nurse ask me what was going on, Lt Called the Nurse and stated inmate appeared to be losing a lot of blood from her private area. Running to dorm E with wheelchair, arrived at the dorm then directed to get a vehicle station wagon carried inmate to the car using sheets and blankets loaded her in the car and proceeded to transport the offender out to the outside hospital.

6/27/90

Assigned to Single cell B Had 15 minute checks on one offender. The Sgt in the building to make rounds and the offender was requesting to talk to them. I went to see what the inmate wanted and carried her some water. The offender asks if she could have her snuff, in which she could not due to her status at the time. Then she said to me just a little pinch of snuff Ms. Ford. Again I told her she could not have snuff. During this time tobacco and snuff were the hot items. It in most cases helps them to keep the inmates calm. Some offenders lived to wake up in the morning and get that pull off that cigarette. Most of the staff just coming on board you can talk to them until you change colors in the face about being undue with an offender. It goes in one ear and out their nose!!! It's terrible.

Women are very unique they like to look good, feel good and be loved by someone, anyone. Women have a different mindset than most men. Most of the time when women are upset they are going to tell someone what's going on with them, usually by this time, there is time to intervene. Talk to other offenders and find out what going on, most of the time stop what is going to happen before it happen.

6/28/90

During line up we were advised by the Captain that there were 3 escapes at Fountain Correctional today, but they were caught and would be transported to NCCIW tonight where they will be house in SCB. Inmates arrived and processed and housed in SCB.

6/30/90

Assigned to dorm H had a confrontation with an inmate who stated God wouldn't forgive her because of some bad things she said to God. God didn't want her to take a shower or comb her hair or eat, stating I'm not going to commit suicide, but what is the need of living. Then she started talking about the Devil.

All the dorms officer desk areas were in the position where if you were talking on the telephone or talking to someone in the building and it was quiet in that dorm those inmates could hear everything you said and they watch everything you done. They made more checks on you than you made on them. Then you would be mad cause you think your friend done put your business out, but actually you did it yourself.

I never wore skirts because I never knew when I may end up in an incident I didn't want to be flashing anyone. SOOOO one night I had no choice my pants were all worn out. I wore a skirt what I do that for. Staff teased and pick at me but I still looked good. I was assigned to lock up that night so I figured ok well I want be seen by many people and no sooner than I walked in that door One inmate set it off yelling to everyone Officer Ford has a skirt on! I switched out with the control person and that's where I was for the remainder of the night.

7/2/90

Was the year they began medicine call and inmates would have to fill out a form to receive medical attention. It was a change and they complained until they got use to it.

7/4/90

Sergeant called me and asks me to come to work due to several staff call in. I told her I could not work. I was on my way home. The sgt ask me where was home I stated Yanceyville. I told her my people were looking for me, because I told them I was coming. I told her if I could come in. I would call and see if they still need me that night.

7/30/90

I was assigned to tower 1 as another officer approached the gate to enter she turn and stated what in the world. I stepped out the tower and heard a lot of yelling loud noise coming from B2. I told Officer to call the sgts office. Then I saw two sgts going to that area. I also went to see what was happening the sgt stated turn the lights on and leave them on. They are locked down, no TV or phone. Someone was making a yelling noise like Tarzan. The Sgt stated someone going to segregation tonight; all the Officer had to do was point her finger at them.

Sergeant talking with an inmate that was about to be released in 73 days after being in prison for 10 years, Inmate was crying and stated she don't know what to do when she gets out. Nowhere to live, no job and can't buy food and she doesn't want to face that.

8/12/90

We were instructed by the Sgt when officer brings in an inmate from anywhere and carrying a weapon, which Officer is not to enter that gate or Tower 1 under any circumstances with a loaded weapon. The Officer is to wait outside the gate until OIC or a supervisor comes and takes control of that weapon before entering that gate. Tower 1 Officer would be responsible for notifying the supervisors.

9/2/90

I was assigned to Tower 1 when a Taxi Cab pulled up about 3:30 am and let out a lady who stated she wanted to see and inmate. I called the supervisors and they came down and talk to the lady. The Lady stated that she had been told by some responsible person that she could see her sister, if she had her driver's license. The Lt. told the Lady she need to leave the premises. The lady stated she didn't have anywhere to go. The Lt Call RPD. Who was there in about 2 minutes they had to be around the corner. Police told her they would have to carry her somewhere she could stay for the night but she refused stating she wanted to see her sister. The lady walked down the street to the stop sign and set on the curve. The lady returned and was again told to leave the premises RPD was called again. The lady finally left and did not return.

9/7/90

I was assigned to dorm D Officer I relieved passed on that there were some problems with a couple of inmates. There was this one inmate just running from room to room being loud and just acting a fool. I ask her what was wrong with her she stated that she had taken some meds earlier that day at the infirmary. This inmate was acting a pure fool. Inmate was attempting to go on the other hall on several occasions. After I completed count inmate had been in several other inmates' rooms. One inmate stated she was in there talking about she wanted some head in here going through her photo album, just sitting here. I don't want her in my room. I got a lot of Gold; I don't want anyone coming in my room stealing my things while I'm sleeping. The next time she comes back in here I'm going to throw her out on her head.

My Supervisor gave me my evaluation which was good. Also recommending me to take the Sergeants examines. The Capt did not have any applications but they would bring me one tonight at lineup.

9/9/90

I was assigned to dorm H inmates being inventoried for court. I was instructed by my supervisors that inmates going to court, state issued clothing are to be packed and store with inmates personal property so when the inmate return, she will not have to be reissued clothing.

11/14/90

At Unit at 7:15 am to ride the van to Butner Umstead Correctional along with several other staff to take the Correctional Sergeants examine. Test began at 9:30 am 4 hours to complete 200 questions. 1:30 pm I was finished. I utilize all my time. It took me about 4 times before I passed but when I passed I knew I passed when I got up because when I looked at my answer sheet it was in a sequence.

12/6/90

I was assigned to the Unit Hospital after Line up I was given my examine letter in which I did not pass.

12/3/90

I was assigned to tower 1 during the morning hours I was advised by medical that EMS had been called and someone would need to open the gate. I immediately called the Lt. and informed them and they said for what! I told her I did not know. Seconds later I observed the Lt. / Sgt tearing out the office going to the unit hospital. Lt had me to get the officer in dorm F to report to infirmary ASAP. Seconds later I observed her running across the yard to the infirmary. The Lt was calling for all available staff to report to area. Officer Ford attempting to get all staff in place before Fire truck / EMS arrives to get gates open. Offender had crossed over in Jordan. The Lt told me as she came through the gate going to the administration building thank you Ms. Ford, you put everybody where they were supposed to be.

Talked with Lt. who asks me if I had tried out for PERT.? I told them yes, when it first started. They stated there was positions open not too long ago but has been filled I told him I would be more than happy to be on PERT. They stated they would let me know when an opening was available, when I ask about getting on PERT, when it first started. I was turned down. It was stated that I would have to have military background or police experience. I look at some of them people that were on there, I knew they didn't have any of that experience.

1991

In the Unit Infirmary heard a commotion going on, walk to the back Officer ask another Officer where was I, the other Officer stated you know where she is. The officer stated I'm not going to do her 8 hrs, I told the Bitch I didn't ask you to do my 8 hrs and she need to keep her damn mouth shut. The officer then stated to me you came in on the ass end of the conversation. I stated no! What it is I just caught your Motherfucking ass talking about me. I was ready to go to her ass. Left and went to talk to the Lieutenant.

Then one night I went into the unit Infirmary to relieve staff for breaks and this Officer was sitting back in the inpatient area TV area, as I walked up I heard her talking about me again. I stood there for a minute and listen and then I popped around the corner and it was if she had swallowed a canary. It went from there and the maintenance man grabbed me by my arm and told me it isn't worth it, it isn't worth it. You had staff that would always keep mess stirred up. It just seemed that all they were there for, sad. That morning when we were scheduled to get off at 6pm Everybody was trying to get to the parking lot, thinking it was going to be a big fight. I got in my car and went home. This individual was a very selfish person that nobody liked I don't care who it was. I always tried to be friendly and respect everyone.

Oh my Goodness Dorm C was the worst building on the compound the water bugs was sooooo big you would be making rounds and they would be crawling all over the inmates. They would be sleep so they didn't know. You would step on them 2 to 3 times to kill them and the sound of them crunching under your shoe. Don't mention when it was about to rain or it was moisture outside they would come running in. I remember one night I was sitting at the desk, I was the only one in there at the time, you know how you just have a feeling about something. I looked up at the ceiling and there was this gigantical ROACH. It's like he just looked at me and said you ready about this time he flew straight at me. If anyone could have seen me trying to get away from that Roach they would still be laughing!!

3/9/1991

To the unit infirmary to relieve Officers and they were in the process of locking down an inmate, being loud yelling and hollering. Once 2nd shift exited I went back to the inmate to find out what was going on with her. I went to her door and she had a piece of metal in her hand. I tried to talk inmate into given me the metal piece, she had already cut her thumb. Inmate would not give it up. The inmate had broken a metal piece of her locker off. The inmate stated when she cut herself it was not going to be her arm, moving the metal piece up and down her arm stating let me find a good vein. We notified the Lts and Sgts what was going on. I went to Segregation building and retrieved the shield. We entered the cell; the inmate claimed she flushed the metal piece. Sgt retrieved the loose bolts and screws from between the wall and the locker.

3/19/91

I was in intake doing fingerprints and IDs on Safe keepers that the county had brought in. One of the Safe keepers didn't have any digits on one hand, so I only did a Thumb and palm print. Later I was told by the LT that anytime something like that happens for each digit missing you write in the fingerprint space digit missing.

I remember one night inmate was disruptive and the sgts call me to come assist along with other staff as we were escorting inmate to dorm c, she fail to comply to orders and pushed the other officer over in the bush (it was so Funny)

11/18/91

I was assigned to B1 in to relieve 2nd shift Officers an inmate was locked up about 9:30 I received a phone call from my supervisor to take over inventory and packing of property. The Officers had only a couple of items left and I told them, if they finish up property I would sign the inventory and take care of the packages. I stated to the Officers they needed to empty the trash and there were a pile of clothes (state) behind the desk on the floor. The Officer stated they were here when they came on. I explain to her anytime something like that is left, she need to inform that staff on duty that she cannot accept the post. If you except it that way then it will be your responsible for the cleanliness of that area.

11/27/91

Went for a Sergeants interview on Wednesday 11:30-12:00

12/18/91

I was assigned to Dorm H 4 Quads with 34 beds in each Quad had some problems with offenders about the telephones. There were about 10 offenders requesting to use the phone from each quad. One offender yelled out to me "no one was to use their phone but them in that quad. I went in the quad and told this offender, she was not going to be yelling through the quad like that. I ran this dorm and I was not going to tolerate her yelling, she don't own or run anything in here. Another offender got mad because I let an offender use the phone, because the number she called was busy. Everyone decide the wanted to use the phone, I informed them I could not satisfy everyone in the dorm between 10-10:30.

12/19/91

Assigned to Dorm F, Inmates not staying in place for count, downstairs C hall very loud and out of order, and inmates all in the hallway. After I did count I told women to go back to their rooms until the count cleared. Cleared count with 2nd shift downstairs inmates look like they were having a parting. I told the inmates I wanted that hall cleared or either they go to their rooms or upstairs in the living area. I had to instruct one inmate a couple of times to not lay her head on another offender. Offender got pissed off, but I could care less.

12/28/91

I was assigned to B1 Total of 75 - 80 inmates to 1 officer, one inmate with a big mouth being loud and rude. I told her I wanted to see her once I finished the count, of course she got loud again as I was changing over with 2nd shift. I cleared the count on B side but A side remained on their beds until they got quiet. I walked back into A side bed area and a inmate ask why they have to stay on their beds because of 1 person. I stated that 1 person makes everybody suffer. I walked back to bed #32 and told the inmate to come with me up front, I wanted to talk to her and she got loud. I told her this was A&B conversation, not the whole Dorm. Inmate asks me do I need to get my shoes. I told her she will be getting them if she doesn't pipe down. After talking with the inmate I had no more problems. There was a Lot of lovers (Couples) in this Dorm housed on the same side. I caught inmate A side back at the lockers. I know they were committing a 23 kissing, but I didn't see them kissing, because when I walked up on them, they didn't know I was there. Before I could get close enough to see them they saw me. With their backs turned to me.

12/29/91

Assigned to B2 working with a newer Officer. Residents were looking at some show on TV and hollered out. The Sergeant called and ask what was going on. I told her nothing and informed her of what was happening. Offenders were getting up going to bed then. Another staff in asking was we alright. I stated we were fine. The officer working with me was about to write up some offenders for hollering. I told the Officer there was going to be times that they would do things and say that you don't like. If you write up an offender, let it be for something that sticks. After that I was again pulled out the building to go do breaks, escorts. Escort the Dining room workers and had to stay because the staff for din room had not shown up for duty. The offenders knew what they were supposed to be doing. I still had to remain because the staff that came in was a male and he couldn't be in there by his self.

12/30/91

Assigned Security Supervisor Relieved 2nd shift Officer informed me
that the offender's records could not be found. I called back to the
unit and advised the Capt. who ask to speak to the Officer. I started
to feeling sick. When I called in my check at 1200 I told my Sergeant
how I was feeling and I was going to try and make it through the night,
but couldn't. So I called back at 2;00 and talk to the Captain and told
her I needed to go home. I explained to her how I was feeling and she
asks would I be able to work the next night because there would be bare
coverage. I told her I would be in but I had to go home tonight, because
I'm sick. Security supervisor when you arrive at the hospital you were
there until someone relieved you the next morning. Break! Either you
would use that restroom in that inmate room or not go. Sometimes
they would send staff out to relieve the staff at the hospital, most of the
time it would be a sergeant.

We had offenders that were on work release. I was sent one night
to transport inmates to Dorthea Dix hosp. I had no idea of how to
get there it want no GPS then. The inmate told me how to get there,
going on inmate told me how to get back to the prison. I was scared
as hell not of the inmate but was she telling me the right direction.
When the inmates come back from work release there was a little like
out house bathroom that we would have to take the inmate in and
shake them down completely. I remember one inmate I shook down I
thought someone had cut her under her stomach when I told my Mom
she started laughing and said she wasn't cut those were stretch marks
and she was right.

The gatehouse that was just a box with glass, Tower 1 was you
received weapons and ammo and your outside equipment. There
was one Ofc they put in the gatehouse all the time and no one knew

that gate house like they did. No Id no entry, they was the Queen of Entrance and Exit.

One night we had an inmate that did not return from work release and it was about a week later we got a phone call stating the inmate had been seen. Lt. told me and another staff come on with me, I had no idea where I was going or whether I was coming back. I know it was downtown at some little hole in the wall club with one way in and one way out on Davie Street. We waited for RPD to arrive. Upon him arriving we went into this club police ofc in front Lt Behind him, one other staff behind her and I was pulling up the rear. Well when we walked in everyone was starring. This one Guy was drunk and as the Police officer approached him he jumped up from his seat in the Police Officer's face. The police officer took his hand and shoved this guy back in his seat. I'm thinking it's time to get the hell out of here! So we did we made our way around and back out but the inmate had gone because someone told her that we were out there.

There was a group of us that after work we hung out together, so one year we planned a beach trip to Mrytle beach we really had a blast. We would go to each other's houses and eat and have fun. This was around the time Women's Empowerment began and everybody would be trying to go. Tom Joyner would be having his outside performances early in the morning downtown.

No One want to work B1 and B2 because they were the worst dorms to work in they didn't bother me. Then there was master control/ Mental Health A1 and A2 -reception all in the same building, no computers COUNT was done by hand. Intake was across the street in a white house looking building. One day this older lady was brought in for housing and she ran from the staff in the building straight to the bathroom and jumped in the toilet feet first and she was just standing there, her feet did look rough. I went to school Basic Training the last week of January and graduated February 24, 1989. Eagle housing was SCB Dorm C mental Health/ Infirmary which was classified as Special housing. B1/B2 A1, A2. were considered A-zone G, F, E, D dorm H were considered B zone staff was assigned to these areas.

Master Control was considered to be A zone, Cardinal Unit was B zone. Dorm H was new and **Phoenix, and Falcon came next and sparrow unit was last.**

There was one staff I couldn't stand to relieve because I felt like they were so mean. You would go in and they would not say anything. You would do your count and tell them what you counted; they would give you the keys and leave. However after getting to know them later in my career they were just as sweet as they could be. I ultimately ended up being their Supervisor when the Falcon Unit opened up, which turned out to be a great working relationship. I was selected as one of the 5 sergeants that opened up the unit. One morning I was sitting in the Sgts office and they came down to the office with 2 inmates and the officer was sooooo upset, because the inmates were down there in the entrance at the doorway having sex. The officer was so upset I had no other choice but to send these inmates to lock up.

I applied for Sgt 7 times and staff was getting promoted and I could not understand why I could not get promoted my job performance was great, I came to work and on time always did what was ask of me. So I wrote a seven page letter to one of the superiors. I was called in and explained my issue and stated that they should just write out a list of names and just pick from the names who they want, there was no need to go by the process of application and interview. This process was so degrading to me. Obviously job performance was not part of the process. I was told that it was political. Everybody knows what that meant. Then I was sent a letter along with race, creed, religion and something else. So the next batch of Sgts which was about 8 and I was in that group. I had asked my supervisor to write a recommendation for me for a sgt position and she told me NO it would not do any good, I told them I would not be giving them any excuses this time around. If I do not get a position I will not apply for another one. I just couldn't understand the staff that was given these positions and I was continuously being look over. I knew what their job performance was because I worked with them as an Officer. Not to say I was perfect but some of the staff promoted was not worth the stripes sewn on their shirt.

There have been very interesting trips to the area hospitals. One trip I remember so very well we were transporting an inmate out that was pregnant that could become irate and because of her custody level. To transport her required a Sergeant and 3 Officers. It was funny because myself and the Sergeant were in the back seat with the inmate between us, officer driving and officer in the passenger. So the inmate started ranting and raving about how she was going to deliver this baby like a woman without no pain medicine, then she started talking to the driver stating I bet you got a weapon don't you and what the officer would do if she tried anything and the officer stated to her yes and I'm a good shot right between the eyes. The inmate never said anything else. The inmate did have to get meds because she could not take the pain as she thought, cursing every minute. This was an Offender that was very unpredictable in most cases. You would know most of the time when she was on her meds and getting ready to strike out at someone. This individual would put on this really RED lipstick and have their face all made up. The next thing we would know she has attacked a staff person. We would hear a code over the radio for the mental health area.

Once we received a code over the radio and when we arrive staff was attempting to restrain a assaultive offender, who hit the sergeant in the head with the door. Once the situation was brought under control, the sergeant was carried to be checked out but could not remember the incident. The offenders in that area could be so verbally abusive to staff and other offenders. You had to sit there and pretty much take it all day.

At the outside hospital with inmate and Dr says she may have to have appendix remove. Well the inmate didn't like that to well, so she stated she was ready to go because she wanted a cigarette. Dr. told her she could have a cigarette. I told him she was not allowed to smoke. Then she stated again she was ready to go. I called the unit and made them aware of what was going on. The Dr didn't want her to leave because they were not sure of her illness, the wanted to keep her overnight and she refused, and she wanted a cigarette. DR told her what would happen if it was her appendix, she still refused. I let the unit know if she was going to stay we would need some assistance because she was going to act a fool. Supervisors arrived with one of the unit nurses, inmate still refuse. Inmate signed a refusal then turned around and signed consent, then refused again. We were given an order that inmate was to remain at hospital. Nurses in trying to get test done inmate tried to bite them. Then we were told by the Administrator at the hospital stated they could not treat anyone refusing to be treated unless they were incompetent.

Another time I was informed that inmate was in Labor by time we got her to our Unit Infirmary and the inmate was sitting in the wheelchair she stated to me its coming! I told her No! Hold on. One thing about being pregnant and in labor that baby is coming! I told infirmary she was getting ready to have this baby as inmate raise her bottom out the chair, when I turned away and turned back it was only a split second the inmate had the baby in her hand WOW!

I was always on a tower or mostly a security supervisor which I enjoyed, I saw my first baby being born, and going out to the hospital with all that equipment on made me feel right proud to be and Officer. When I was on the tower the Supervisors were supposed to come out to each tower and check on the staff but instead they would stand in a particular spot and flash their flash light at you and you were supposed to flash back at them. So whenever I was on the tower I would see them flashing but I would not flash back. Then they would have to walk all the way out to the tower and make sure I was ok They would be some kind of mad at me when they came to the tower and I was standing at the door. Most of the staff out normally would be non-alert. Then there was one Officer talking about she had seen a fly saucer twice. So they never put her back on the tower again.

One time I carried out an inmate and when you go out there they always put a ID bracelet on inmate arm, so when we returned to the facility and inmate was place back in her housing I forgot to remove the bracelet and the inmate did not want to give it up. So when we went to get the bracelet off inmate in the cell the inmate dipped in the toilet and threw liquid (PEE) on me. Well as I proceeded in the cell with other staff to obtain the hospital bracelet, I lost my glasses but I was holding my own. The Sgt was down on the floor looking for my glasses under the cell bed but she couldn't find then and the inmate stated "I broke them Bitch" I said ok. The inmate complained about her stitches being busted. The Sgt found my glasses and they exited followed by myself that was a vital lesson to me, However the bracelet was retrieved. There was never a boring minute it was always something to get the adrenaline rush.

I carried an inmate out to outside hospital one night it was so many people in ER that night. Most of the time we would have to wait due to people coming in on the ambulance and this particular night the nurse stated to me that there were to trauma patients coming in that were in a motorcycle accident, they said the drivers were playing chicken. I was like HUH! They said yes that's a game they play on the motorcycle when you are facing each other at a high rate of speed and neither chicken out so they collided. That's terrible!!

Another time a younger inmate (Safekeeper) was put in the cell with regular population inmate and the inmate refused to move out the cell well the inmate ended up biting me on the shoulder. as several other staff stood behind me an watch her bite me I will never forget. We did move inmate to another cell. I was so angry because staff just stood there watch this inmate biting me and done nothing. My Lt. told me you better be worried about whether that inmate HIV or not. I was bit really hard but the skin was not broken. I did fill out a WC4 and was checked. I was the type of Officer I did my job and when the Capt or Lt asks I would tell them the task is done. We had transfers and property then to that had to be carried to intake.

I had Officers that didn't want me to talk to certain staff because they didn't like them. I explained to then I cannot dislike someone I don't know just because they didn't like them. There was one Officer that no one seems to like but she and I got along good for the most part. I then left the infirmary and went to the Capt / Lts office that was between the now dorm C and the dining room a little match box. Dorm C oh my Goodness was a dungeon, usually one officer with about 80 beds. The Cock roaches were so big you were scared to step on them. My self and the Sgt went in the dorm C warehouse one night looking for property and we saw the bag moving, I told Sgt. It's got to be a snake the way the bag was moving. Sgt said to be sure not. When we removed the bag there were like a Thousand roaches in a bag with food that had been put in the warehouse. This is when Memo came out no perishable food items were to be placed in the warehouse. All these items had to be replaced through the inmate welfare fund was what it was called back then.

One morning a friend of mine was taking me home to my Moms in Yanceyville to pick up my vehicle 1976 Ford Elite. It was raining bad that morning as we were on the out skirts of Hillsborough, it felt like the tires on the car were slipping, in my mind I was like what is that why does the car keep doing that, not knowing 5 minutes later we were in a accident and when the car starting slipping this time it didn't stop until after we hit a ditch. I could see where we were going so I braced myself up out the seat with my arms and hands for the impact. The Highway Patrolman was sitting on the other side of the road with another accident and watched us crash. When I got out the car I was shaking so badly, I could not stand up. Police officer ask me was I ok I told him yeah I'm trying to get myself together. Well I Call for my Mom to come get us but I couldn't get her so I call a friend of the family and told them, I had been in an accident but I was ok, I needed someone to come pick us up in Hillsborough. My Mom was contacted and came and picked us up. We went to Yanceyville and picked up car and came back to Raleigh, not knowing my friend had totaled their car. When we hit the ditch it knocked a hole in the floor board on the passenger side where I was sitting, the impact was so great. I returned to Raleigh didn't go to the Dr cause I did want to cause damage to their insurance. Well it didn't matter the car was totaled and the insurance went so high they had to get insurance somewhere else. Meantime our crazy asses went to work that night. I was hurting so bad I could barely walk. Our Supervisor asks what was wrong with me and I told them the story. They ask me why was I at work, I told them because not moving was going to make it worst. Our Supervisor sent us home I was in bad shape. I got home I still didn't lie down because I knew I was not going to be able to move. I did everything I could besides lay down. I worked that soreness out my body.

One night I came to work and I had the toothaches that just make you want to walk out in front of a car. I hurt so badly that night and I ask my Supervisor could I go home because I felt like I was dying. So she let me go home I took some meds and the mouth calmed down. Oh well up jump the devil about two months later. I told my supervisor I had a toothache they said to me I thought you went to the dentist and had that tooth pulled. I said no I didn't because it stopped bothering me. So this time I was allowed to leave I was told to go get that shit pulled out, you come back to work with that tooth in your mouth I'm going to pull it myself. Eventually I did have it pulled.

Working in Dorm F we had to work A/B and C hall down stairs most of the time you were by yourself with a full dorm of inmates. The only area I never work at Women's prison was the Phoenix unit. I work at the gatehouse and when Inmate would come in from work release we had to search then and the night I search this inmate I said to myself oh my goodness this lady had been abused she looks like she had been cut in her stomach, when I told my Mom she laughed and said no those were stretch marks from having a baby.

One time there were two officers sent out to security supervise and inmate at the hospital and the relieve the night shift staff and before night shift returned the officers called and stated that the inmate was gone. The inmate walked out of a two way bathroom in the emergency room that morning and the Officers had no idea they were sitting there waiting on the inmate to come out the restroom. When they opened the door they discovered there was another door and the inmate was gone. Needless to say what happen after that? I don't think that inmate was ever captured.

Back then inmates were allowed to stay up all night and watch TV on the weekends and holidays. At this time the Phoenix Unit was in the process of being built. Dorm H had recently been finished and this was where new admissions would be housed and pregnant inmates. Old A1, 2 Housed reception/ pregnant inmates along with this was where Master Control was located and Mental Health. I enjoyed being an Officer and was proud of it. At the time there was only one Capt. There was one Officer that could get her every time when they got in trouble all they had to do was talk about cooking rabbit and squirrel and she would completely forgot about what everything they done. They were a fast talker to. LOL.

I was assigned as the Control Officer in SCB that was when everything mostly worked the control board opening and closing gates verses now and nothing works. Years ago we were never allowed to keep the gates open due to safety issues and assaultive inmates. Then if something stops working you would have to control it manually. Now the mindset is well we will just leave it open instead of going through all that opening and closing. Then inmates had figure out how to come out the cells undetected.

Working in lockup Administration Segregation which is now called (restrictive housing 2016) I was assigned as one of the floor officers where it was always loud and noisy inmates yelling, talking from side to side. Talking to the air vents to their friends or just cursing someone out. I always tried to be attentive and listen for odd noises or things out the ordinary. I was sitting there and I heard a clicking noise and this would always happen after I have made my rounds on the floor. So this went on for a couple of days while I was assigned to that area. I was determined I was going to find out what that noise was. So what I did was after I made my rounds on the floor I back tracked very quietly and when I heard the noise I immediately went to that hall and there I found that the inmates where manipulating the locks on the doors and coming out of their cell going to other cells to visit. When I saw the inmate in the hallway I said hey get back in that cell. The inmate chuckled and ran back to her cell saying you caught me. I stated to them you all been doing this a long time haven't you, but no longer. After that metal strips were placed on the doors to keep them from manipulating the locks. Inmates were using a flat piece of anything to stick in the door to pull back the lever which would open the door. Maintenance placed a metal piece over the doors to prevent tamper by inmates.

1991

The State bureau of investigations had been out to the prison on several different occasions. You never knew when you were under an investigation. You would know when you were being questioned. This particular time an investigation was being conducted an ultimately ended with a Supervisor being escorted out and being prosecuted in court. It was so disturbing to me. I was just in disbelief that this was happening to this Supervisor, in order for it to take place it had to be some evidence. It was so degrading to have them escorted through the yard for everyone to see staff and inmates. Since then there have been quite a few escorted out.

Inmates have a certain time they are supposed to be in their night gowns and robes, so I had instructed one lady that's what she needed to do, another inmate walked up and ask to go inside the bed area and get some water. When I open the door she stated I don't want to go now and sat back down on the couch. When I got up to open the gate for another inmate the same inmate asking to go earlier tried to go in the bed area, I closed the gate. She thought that was cute. I don't have time for that shit!

This same inmate made the statement to me one night do not come back in the bed area because there were women not clothed and indecent. I felt as though inmate was making an insinuation as far as I could see and hear. I did not respond I continued to make my check. Inmate was standing at another inmate's bed and I instructed her she needed to go to her own bed. I again stated you are not to be at another inmate's bed sitting or talking. I was talking to another inmate an instructed the inmate again to go to her bed. The inmate stated to me you need to leave out the bed area. I continued making my rounds. Inmate later came to the desk and asks for a sick call sheet and sat down in the chair by the open gate and as I started to walk through the gate to make my check, the inmate acted like she was going to hit me. I didn't flinch just kept walking and inmate finally went to bed.

Then we made a lot of overtime due to being short, so one of the supervisors ask me could I work on Saturday, I told her no and she stated to me some damn body got to work. I told them if they could not get anybody else to work I would. So another Officer wanted to work Saturday and be off Sunday so I told them I would work Sunday and they would work Saturday for coverage.

I exit the prison one day and I was so angry, I tried to take my frustration our on my car which was a 1975 gold tone Ford Elite with a 351 Cleveland motor. Well it almost took me out when I when down that hill driving crazy and when I try to stop at the stop sign, I literally stood up and the brakes to stop and this car kept sliding right though the 4 way stop. All the other cars just sit there and looking at me, needless to say I never try that stunt again after scaring the HELL out myself.

1/3/92

Assigned to B2 11:05 had some offenders to get upset because I turn down the TV. I explain to them if they did not make so much noise, they could hear. If they get quiet I will turn the TV back up, because they were not the only ones in the building. I had another offender to come to the TV area fussing and mumbling. So I ask the offender what was her problem? She stated to me that another offender had something of hers and she wanted it back. I obtained the offenders name and went to her bed and ask her did she have something that belong to someone else, at first she said NO. So I told the offender if she had something that belong to someone else she need to return it, because I would hate to see bought of them go to lock up over something petty.

12:10 another offender out of the bed area to smoke a cigarette, I told her she needs to go back to her bed, she ask for what? Offender appeared to upset, offender set at table and smoked. Offender requesting Mental Health medication, offender along with another was escorted to receive their medications. I informed the Sgts office that a lot was going on in these dorms, the Officers are not doing their jobs. Then the Lt. Went into this long song and dance. We did come to an understanding about smoking once the offender leaves the TV area there will be no smoking only in the TV area. So I took it upon myself to write down a list of when certain rules and times were applied at night. Carried it to the Sgts office let them review and I was instructed to run copies off for uphill dorms B1, B2, and A2. 2 Copies per dorm 1 posted on bulletin board and officer has access to a copy.

1/8/92

I was assigned to Dorm G relieving 2nd shift conducting count and the Sergeant had me to report back to her to transport an inmate and she told me once they admitted her and she was placed in a room, I could return to the unit because she was a min II custody. Another sergeant ask me to go by and check on another inmate that was already at hospital and make sure no one was in her room with her, her family has been staying with her all night. One night I was sent out to the area hospital to check on inmates that at that time did not require Security Supervisors and when I entered the room on the maternity floor were the inmate had a baby there was a lady sitting in the room in the rocking chair with the baby rocking. I ask where was the inmate and she gave all these excuses. I ask who was she and she stated that she was the inmates Mom. I continued to ask questions. After about 30 mins the inmate had not returned, I called back to the institution and talked with my Sgt. and told her that the inmate was not there and she said what do you mean she not there and she is not here. The Sgt. Then stated several choice words. This inmate had left the hospital in her Moms car and went to Fayetteville to get high over night and then returned by 0600 am as if she was in the hospital all the time sitting in the waiting area of the hospital. The inmate knew as long as she was not gone 24 hrs she would not be considered and escape and would not be charge.

1/31/92

PERT call out received call from our Lt. @ women prison.

2/1/92

@ 11:00 reported to Central Prison assembly room addressed by administration. Deployed to women's prison 1st and 2nd Platoon. Lt announced a Code 100 Escape. We would and did move in to complete a search of the entire unit looking for anything especially USI weapon used to enter from the back of the 208 building. Teams were then disbursed to different dorms. I was on the first team which went to Dorm D. All offenders were placed in the dayroom, 2 officers to a room male /female. Offenders were searched and called to their rooms while being their personal belonging was searched. This was repeated until the entire unit was searched.

2/8/92

Assigned to Tower 1 Security Supervisors waiting to go to hosp 1 officer came in to wait for the other 2 officers to arrive. So another officer arrived and I provided her with information and car keys. The officer then came into tower 1 and was going to stand there til 5:45. I stated to the Officer that all of them could not come in Tower 1 and sit down. The Officer stated all of who? There is nobody but her and the other officer. I stated you can't stay in Tower 1 and the officer said well I'm not standing out in the cold. My supervisors don't expect me to stand out here in 17 degree weather. I stated to the officer she had the car keys, she could go start the car up so it could be warming up. The officer stated to me she was not supposed to leave until 5:45. I stated to her it didn't make any difference to me what time she left, but she was going to get out of here. The officer then became loud seemed upset. I'm not upset I'm just not going to stand out here in the cold. I told her she was not going to stand in here. So the other officer finally got up and left out and this officer followed. They went out and could not find the car that was assigned to them. I yelled out to them it was the first car as you walk out the gate. The officer comes back to Tower 1 and states to me I'm aware I'm a security supervisor but who am I setting with. I told her I gave you all the information, what did you do with it? it was in her hand. This is just one DINGBAT!!!

2/14/92

Assigned to Infirmary Door Once I had changed over with my officer at the door, I went back to assist the inpatient officer with clearing the count in that area. When the officer finished her count it was not right. I went with the officer to count again. There were a lot of doors open that should be locked and were not locked by the 2nd shift officer. While recounting the officer at the door called and stated that Mental Health officers were ready to go. I stated they were just going to have to wait. After the count cleared in our area the door officer called stated MH officers called again. I told her I can't help that they have to wait. The officers stated they were going to call the Sgts office, I told them they could call the Sgts office and anybody else they wanted to call on this compound. If she wanted to get out that bad jump the fence. So then medical had something to say. I told them I'm doing my job, I'm going to do it right and no one will stop me and that goes for them as well. I do what I need to do and no one will get through that gate because I have the keys. I reported all of what occurred to my supervisor. I tried to explain to medical that all rooms not being occupied at the change of shifts need to be secured and once the shift has change the break area would be reopened.

2/22/92

Assigned to outside hospital taking out an offender who was in labor. I advised my Capt. that I had pulled a muscle in my back and ask her to send someone else out to the hosp. I told her I couldn't go. I was in a lot of pain. The Capt stated to me well it probably will be better for me, because I would not have to do a lot of moving about. So I transported the offender out. 12:45 the offender was returned to the unit. Upon my arrival to the unit trying to get out the car the automatic locks were not working. I had to open the front doors manually. Once I exited the vehicle the door locks were still not functioning. So now HOUSTON we got a big problem. I could not get this offender out the backseat although l attempted several times. I had Tower 1 to advise the Sgts of what was going on. I continued talking to the offender and at the same time trying to figure out how to get these doors open. Told the offender don't worry we were going to get her out the car; she seemed pretty calm at 4.00 centimeters in her labor. Another staff came to assist. I told the officer I think a fuse may have blown, because the vehicles horn and lights on inside are not functioning. I then ask the officer to switch the fuses at least long enough for me to get the offender out the back seat of the car. When the officer made the switch of the fuses everything was functioning long enough for us to remove the offender, about 10 secs and the fuse blew again. On the 24th I received a letter from management thanking me for a job well done and taking the lead in this situation. My Capt stated to me after she gave me the letter don't let anyone else read that because it's sure to cause some jealousy. I was relieved from Single cell to go to Dorm F. While making rounds, I came to the dayroom area and notice a lot of couple offenders were in the area. Two sets of couples sitting on the sofa. One of the offenders was sitting on sofa with her knees up and her robe draped across her. I continued to observe and at that point I feel as if something sexual was going on. I walked up to them and told them they needed to separate and sit up. The offender made a statement "what do you mean. I told her to sit up and take that robe from over her knees and put it on.

3/7/92

One night I was assigned to Tower 6, and this car drove up I did not come out of the tower, I stood there to watch and see what the guy was going to do. The vehicle set at the gate for about 5 minutes and immediately tried to back up and back into the ditch. The driver tried to spin the back end of the car out the ditch. The driver got out the car and tried to push the car out the ditch. The driver was so intoxicated he did not know where he was and urinated right there. The driver then approached the gate and threw up his hands. I never came outside. The driver then went back to the car and tried to spin out again. He then got out of the car and started walking away from the vehicle. I again notified supervisors. I call my supervisor and informed them of what was happening they called RPD. RPD arrived I gave them needed information. Then the driver returned he was arrested and carried away Later the DA contacted me and stated this individual would be going back to court and I would probably be subpoenaed if so she was going to release me from that, but ask if I could be on standby in case she needed me. So I told my supervisor what she said. My supervisor said what release you from the subpoenaed, she said not if you get that subpoena to go to court. Unless the DA could give you some signed document releasing me. The DA could forget she told you that and then you would go to jail. NO NO NO!!! I'm not going to jail. Needless to say I never heard anything else about it.

3/15/92

Assigned to Tower 1 working my night off. Line up being held the Lt. called out codes and ask me what a code 100 was. I said a fight. I knew better, but I could not think of escape. I knew what it was but I could not say it.

3/16/92

I was assigned as relief officer my name was not called out on the line up. Capt told me to remain in the office. Later began relieving for breaks. To single cell with the Sgts due to offender having items covering up the door and window in her cell. After wakening up the offender and talking to her, she removed the items with no problems. Conducting escorts to dining room insulin and Ramadan. Radio Dorm E officer repeatedly to send out her ladies. The officer called out to me and stated for me to call the Sgts office. I did talk to the Sgt and she stated to me that I don't need to say ladies on the radio. I ask the Sgt what she want me to use inmates. Sgt told me you do to suit yourself. I told Sgt I could pick them up at the dorm and not use the radio. Sgt stated again you do to suit yourself and hung up the phone on me. After escorting I went to the Sgts office and talk to Sgt and told her I wanted her to tell me how to talk on the radio, then an officer started talking. I stated to the officer, I don't want you to tell me I want the Sgt to tell me. Sgt stated maybe, you should get another sgt to tell you. I stated NO I want you to tell me. Sgt stated just what I said I ain't going to bite my tongue to say it again. I got right up in her face and ask her if she had holes in her tongue, I wanted to see them. We all fell out laughing!

The old stockroom where we went to get our uniforms the officer working there was very particular about that area; don't go in that area because she would know someone had been the rummaging through her inventory. They could always size you up before you would ask for your size in uniform "here try these on, you look like you can where this size."

3/17/92

Assigned to Tower 6 Sgt in the stockroom (which was a large old building) later torn down. I saw the Sgt come out and go down to the ramp and appeared to be doing something, but I could not see for the tree. Even after I did not see the Sgt leave, she called and asks me did I see her. I ask where at the stockroom. Sgt stated yes she was jumping up and down, came around to tree and up to the gate. Sgt ask me was I sleep. I told her no, I didn't see her anymore after she left the ramp at the stockroom. Sgt stated ok long as you seen me doing something. Once I was relieved for break I ask Sgt about the equipment in Tower 6. The equipment should be logged by number on the equipment sheet. Sgt stated Lt. told her long as what supposed to be there is there, don't worry about it. Sgt stated she was not worried because she had talked to Lt. Time and time again. I stated just because he stated that don't mean its right.

8/10/92

I was assigned at tower 1 3:10 am I observed a Taxi Cab going into the parking lot and then a few minutes later approach Tower -1 I white female got out the vehicle, I ask how can I help you after she approached the gate, she stated she was looking for the main prison. I told her she was at the main prison, she said no, the main prison is downtown, she continued on and on. I called and notified my supervisors of what was going on who sound like she was disturbed. The lady stated she was from Fayetteville and the cab driver verified that information. Supervisor called RPD because the woman sounded like she really needed help. Raleigh PD arrived after talking to the cab driver and the lady RPD lead the cab off the premises.

8/11/92

I was wrapping packages to be mailed out and I discovered that my supervisor daughter was there as a new admission for obtaining property with a worthless check.

8/23/92

In the Capt/Lts office to get me some coffee as I was leaving Lt. called me I turned around and she started shaking the money jar at me. Lt stated to me I needed to put some money in the jar. So she really pissed me off by her tone of voice. I told her there have been times that I came in there and put $2.00 in the jar. I come get a cup of coffee and you gone beg me for a dime. I told her Oh No! Lt stated that the Sgt put her in charge of the coffee. Lt told me I need to talk to the Sgt, I told her no I don't. So I put a quarter in the damn jar and told her to have a good night, not that I cared. So I was talking to the Sgt about my 113 time sheet. The Lt Calls the Sgt and tells her what I said. I told her I don't even won't the fucking coffee. I went and poured it out in the sink. So the Sgt was telling me well you know a lot of people come and get coffee but don't put money in the jar. I told her when I come get coffee it's a lot said, I put money in the jar. I ask her how many times a night do they get coffee and don't put money in the jar. I left and went to employee break area. Then I had to return to get trash bags and another Sgt said how many you need. I told her they were for Tower 6. They said well I don't have that many. I said fine it's not like I want them for my personal use, just give me one. Everyone else can worry about themselves.

9/11/92

Lt. called me and ask me if I knew how long it took to get to the airport. I told her about 15 or 20 mins, she tells me I have a task for you. I want you to take this inmate to the airport and make sure she gets on the plane. I picked up inmate and escorted her to the office when she change clothes and was given her money from her trust fund account $5,980.45. The Sgt counted out 5 stacks of 10 $100.00 bills, 980.00 and .45 cents. The inmate took the money that she was going to by her plane ticket 490.00 From 500.00. The other money was in an envelope with a rubber band around it; put it in her right front pocket. Escorted inmate to RDU airport walked her to the gate where she was to board the airplane. I think she was going to California.

9/23

I was assigned to the Unit Infirmary and offender was cursing and being loud as usual; she had set herself on fire earlier that day and had severe burns. On her bed bragging about all the important people were there, when she set herself on fire.

10/4/92

Out to hospital with an inmate who went out earlier on ambulance, I was told she may be trying to escape. Retrieved all my equipment and transported offender out along with another Officer. Hospital security was notified prior to our arrival and met us in emergency room. Security notified us there were to more people in the ER with that same last name as the inmate. Security escorted us to a room and inmate was secured appropriately. Hospital staff seems to think offender was faking. Officer with me stated that inmate stated to her she needed help, help get her out of there. I called the unit and informed the Sgt of everything going on, she stated to me that she was sending an officer with a weapon. I talked to security and ask who the other 2 people were and one was an 11 year old black girl and a black male who was drunk he was just drunk or appeared to be that way. Inmate was finally seen and was returned to the unit I radioed the unit and let them know we were in the vehicle and returning to the unit.

1/93

I was assigned to dorm F relieved staff for 2nd shift 3 of the ladies were on their way to lock up Dorm C. C/o caught two lady's in another lady's room and one was under the bed with no clothes on. Then the inmate under the bed and the inmate whose room she was in to commit a sexual 23 act got into a confrontation.

1/9/93

We had received information that a load of Dope was coming through on Sunday during visitation.

1/16/93

Received a new admission back from Escape in 1975. The Capt ask me to go assist the Sgt. because she felt like the admission might flip out. So I went back and assisted and completed the finger prints and ID while the Sgt completed the paperwork. The admission was then escorted to medical.

I returned back to dorm F, where the other officer called and ask if she could go do breaks. There were a few Ladies still in the dayroom area watching TV, at 2:00 am I had them to clean up the area. 6 or 7 of them had ganged up in the bathroom. I told them to come out. Then all of them stated they had to use the bathroom. I went back; I told all them I wanted them out of that bathroom NOW!! They all scattered. It took a while for things to calm down. They finally calm down and appeared asleep. Officer returned and I then went with the newer officer to escort Din Room ladies. So when we got to the din room the officer didn't have the key to open door. I went to the office and ask the sgt why they keep sending these officers to escort to the din room but don't give them a give them a key. The Sgt was sitting there with the key in her pocket.

1/26/93

Lt. had summoned me to the office and ask me if I wanted to be acting Sgt. of course I accepted and they assigned me to special housing, of course the other staff was tripping. Then one of our problem children needed to go to medical because of a complaint of chest pains. Lt called and ask me if she needed to send the Sgt over if we had to go into the cell. I told Lt I had two Officers on the floor that I felt they would stand behind me if anything jumped off. When I told the Officers what the situation was they stated no problem. Entered cell with no problems and exited. I enjoyed being an officer and I was glad that I got to train with the old school, because I watched them and studied them and learned how to deal with certain different situations. It was always a learning experience. Working in this environment tamed me a great deal. Dealing with the inmates and them cursing you out and calling you all kinds of names, I had to figure out a way to deal with it and not react or lose my job. Most of the staff thought I was out of some branch of the military because of the way I carried myself.

SERGEANT

JANUARY 21, 1993

I was promoted to Correctional Sergeant. Thank the LORD!!!!

2/8/93

I received some mail from an individual from my hometown that was admitted. I had to write a statement and call her in to talk with her per the Lt and let her know the rules and the policy. I brought the lady in and talked to her in the presence of other supervisors and let her know it probably would be in her best interests if she did not broadcast she knew me, because others would think I was doing her favors and that she could be written up and go to disciplinary for such an act. (Have written letter)

2/10/93

Training other staff how to bring in new admissions Finger prints /ID.

2/13/93

To Dorm F to relieve an officer who became sick and had to talk to an inmate because she wanted Pine sol to clean her room at 11:00 tonight I advised her she is only to clean her room during the day shift hours not on 3rd shift. No! She could not have any pine sol. Another inmate requesting to move because her roommate doesn't take showers and she is filthy, I advised her to she needed to talk day shift because we don't make movements on 3rd shift.

Inmate making complaint that a Sgt was going to lock her up because she would not give up her bottom bunk, but inmate had a medical excuse for a bottom bunk, then inmates had to have medical notes for a bottom bunk / bed board or a T- shirt which was very hard to come by. Now you can't even get find a bottom bunk, bed board or T-Shirt because everyone has a medical note.

2/16/93

Sgt Ford and Officer to Central Prison (CP) to gas up vehicles for chapel hill/Durham hospitals. Officer on tower 6 called and stated there were 6 supervisors going out. He had only 4 weapons. Lt advised that Chapel Hill will pick up weapons from tower 6 and Durham and wake will change over at the hospital. Officer on T-6 made a statement about the weapons being switched over at the hospital. Senior Sgt which to me was over everything stated there is to be no exchanging weapons at the hospitals. If there are not enough weapons a Sgt will have to go to T-6 and check out weapons from downstairs in the vault.

3/1/93

Sgt Ford and another Sgt escorted an inmate out to the Hospital because she had intentionally swallowed a fingernail clipper, penny and a paperclip, then stated to us that she would refuse treatment. Upon us arriving to see medical they told us that she would go to Mental Health across the street. The other Sgt called back to the unit and the Capt. told us to bring the inmate back to the facility. Arrived back at the unit inmate was placed on suicidal precautions.

3/3/93

Relieved 2nd shift officers, inquired about the 141's that had been completed. The officers stated they didn't know about it and it was left by third shift. I advised them regardless of the shift it was on they were the ones being held accountable. They need to take care of it before they left.

3/4/93

Officer assigned to Tower 1 reported that two armed men near the chapel area firing weapons. Sgt Ford reported this to the Capt. the Capt told me to tell Officer to return to Tower 1, RPD Raleigh Police Department would be here shortly, they had been called. Officer will need to talk to RPD once they arrive. Officer talked with RPD. Tower 6 Officer was notified due to RPD going to that area. Afterwards RPD left the institution and did not return.

3/9/93

In dorm G to dorm for a so called gas leak, I entered the laundry room where I could smell some type of fluid as if it was coming from the dryer. They were clothes in the dryer that had a cigarette lighter that exploded. I told the Officer just let the dryer stand with door open the remainder of the night. Another Sgt and I had talked with some inmates who stated another inmate was telling them that I Sgt Ford was related to her, I was her Aunt. I talked to the inmate with the other Sgt present and told her if she was doing this she needed to stop; she could get a write up behind it.

3/13/93

Working B zone down the hill to make rounds. Door banging at the New Building Phoenix unit, had officer to go with me and we secured the door.

3/19/93

Officer in dorm D called in reference to an inmate that was determined to dry her clothes after 11 pm. I told the Officer I was leaving to her to handle. 10 min later the officer called me back stating the same inmate had started up the dryer again, it was 11:30 pm I told the officer I was on my way down to Dorm D. I talked to the Officer and then the inmate. During this time the inmate had left the clothes in the dryer. Someone turned the drier on while we were in conference in the office. By the time we got done talking the inmate went to the laundry room to get her clothes and the dryer was on, she came back and ask the officer did she know the dryer was on, in which we didn't by this time the clothes were pretty dry.

Two inmates had come in to talk to me due to another inmate, stating she had been crying all day. Inmate had been to Mental Health but she would not talk to any of them about what was going on. I talked with her and she was explaining that there was an issue going on with her child. I ask her if she had any sleep, she stated no, not since the day before. I ask her was she going to work in the Din Rm, she stated she had no choice. I told her that I would talk to the Supervisor in the Din Rm tell her not in detail but that you been upset and hadn't had any rest and the inmate stated ok. The officer was then telling me that there was nothing substantial to go by in waking up inmates to go to work in the Din Room. I went and talked to the din room Supervisor and let them know we need a list to go by to wake up din room inmates. The supervisor stated to me that the list changes every week starts on Mon go til Sun. I told them we would need to get a copy of the list every Sunday for our dorm G officers so will have something substantial to go by so we will know who is to be release for the din room. Inmates signing their names on a piece of paper to be awakened are not enough for me, because an inmate could attempt an escape like that.

3/21/93

Raleigh Correctional bringing in inmate for medical. Inmate appeared to be balling up her fist anytime staff approached her. Inmate was escorted for a medical check. Once the inmate found out she was going to lock up, she appeared to be upset and vulgar. Once in lock up area she stated I'm going to have someone job. Inmate was then instructed to get in cell and she refused several times and then complied. Inmate did not want to give up her clothing but did later, asking to talk to SBI agent. The Senior Sgt ask me what were the 2 things that need to occur when someone goes to lock up. I told her inventory of the property and complete a DC-193.

3/22/93

I was assigned to special housing Inmate being transported from Raleigh and escorted to medical Mental Health. During the same time another inmate causing disruption in the Phoenix Unit was being escorted up to medical thinking there would be problems with this individual, instead another inmate from the Phoenix Unit refused her housing in medical (MH) Did a lot of talking with the inmate she to get her in cell, now to get her clothes, earrings, nose. All items were obtained without incident. Inmate in Dorm C refusing to take her meds, I talked with inmate and asked her what was the reason she did not want to get her meds, she stated she didn't want to be in handcuffs. I told her this was procedure. I told her to get up and slip her clothes on and I would escort her to get her meds and back to dorm C.

3/25/93

Hepatitis vaccine taken oh man you talk about something that hurt for days. Back to inpatient area and the Officer ask when inmates were to be in bed. I told her they are to be in bed at 10:00 pm. The TV goes off at 9:30 pm unless special permission is granted. 11:40 inmate complained that she was moved off her bottom bunk, another inmate was assigned to her bed and she was assigned to a top bunk. I told inmate unless you have a bottom bunk medical, it was nothing that could be done. Inmate stated I have a bad back. I informed her she need to be seen by medical, fill out sick call request.

3/30/93

Assigned to special housing making rounds in Single cell had a little training with dorm C, and S/C the Officers had to show me how to use a full pair of restraints.

4/9/93

Returned back to work from vacation and I was told that the only Sgt/ Lt that knew how to run 3rd shift and I shadowed was placed on 2nd shift. DAMN!

Another Lt that was on shift assigned me 3 new Trainees. I was informed I would need to do 30 day interims on the Officers until they go to permanent status. I was provided with a PMS pkg, ran off several copies 1 for Officers what their duties consist of.

Then we had what was called Permanent Status. Entries would be kept on the new employee every month for 6 months or a year. You would appear in front of a board of three members and they would look at your Performance Management System (PMS) Not a women thing OK! This board of people would determine if you were ready to become a permanent employee or be extended.

Received a call from Officer who stated they saw something moving down by the Phoenix Unit. Myself and an Officer down to the area but did not see anything unusual. Advised Tower #2 #3 to keep an eye out, if they see anything contact me, Arrived back at the office talked to one of the new officers that was assigned to me and she told me that her brother was at Harnett Correctional as an inmate, but she had already informed the Lt.

Lt appointed me as the Safety Officer for 3rd shift. Being relieved by 1st handcuff key missing from key box and could not be accounted for, by A Zone Sgt. I called Tower #6 who had 5 and should only have 4. Officer brought extra key to me and it was placed in the key box.

4/21/93

Assigned special housing Sgt, Molring on unit In Infumary Unen had not been removed of bed, ask the Lt. who stated that it is the responsibility of the nurses to clean those areas. Needless to say when 1st shift came in they would not relieve my staff because of the bed linen still on the bed. The other Lt. stated tell the staff to clean it up in which I did. I told the Lt. I would do it because I was the one that told her don't worry about it. I told the Lt I would go over there and make sure it was done and the Lt. stated to me and don't you go over there and do it either. To infirmary cleaned up room picked up trash with the officer's assistance. So when I returned to the office the Lt. as me did I do it and I told her "yes", she stated to me so you disobeyed a direct order. I stated I show did, she yells out to me as I was walking out the door, I will deal with that tonight. I told her that's fine I will be here Advised the staff assigned to Mental Health to check their doors, I found 2 doors unsecure.

4/22/93

Assigned to special Housing did a little training with my staff asking them about Fires/fire hazards. I ask staff at what point do you let an inmate out of a cell. I informed them I was advised by the Lts. that no matter if the inmate was violent. You as DOC employees is here for safety and security of that individual. You have to open that door and let that individual out of that cell. When I talked with other staff regarding Fires and told them the same thing they did not feel comfortable with that.

4/26/16

Assigned to special housing along with another Sgt. the Sgt working B Zone went and complain to the Lt. about working that area and the Lt moved the Sgt working with me and put her in B zone instead.

5/6/93

I was assigned to A-Zone -busy night court trips being call to be escorted to go eat in din room, due to them exiting at 4:30 am. Then had to deal with an unruly resident.

5/12/93

Assigned A-Zone received a call from the Cardinal Unit Sgt that she would be bringing up a resident who sometimes could be very unruly to Mental Health. Resident was refusing to be escorted Sgt and Officer escorted her. Lt and other Sgts ask shouldn't that resident had on handcuffs. I called the Sgt once they were at their destination and ask why the resident was not escorted in handcuffs. The Sgt stated resident said if I got to go in handcuffs then you are going to have to fight me. After the resident was escorted to mental health and back to her dorm she requested to see me. I went down to dorm G and was informed that a resident was supposed to be bringing drugs in after visitation by swallowing a balloon and then make herself throw up once she got back to the building. Reported all this information to the Lt. the Lt. ask me did I tell the Sgt about the handcuffs, I told her yes, what was wrong with that. So the Lt stated to me what did we talk about in the meeting the other night? What is discussed between Lt. and Sgt supposed to stay that way? I told Lt. I did see anything wrong with me telling the Sgt what she said. Lt. stated well I wanted to tell her. I told the Lt. you don't have to worry about talking to her now. So I told the Lt. How about from now on I just keep my mouth shut.

A letter was left at Tower #1 To Whom It May Concern written on it. Gave the letter to the Lt who opened it and it read that a resident had objects in her cell.

The Lt. was just a DAMN nuisance tonight sitting at the switch board and couldn't even get her tail up and open the gate for staff. The Lt Then made the statement your Sgt has the key. I laid the key on the desk in front of her because I was on the telephone and stated your Lt got them now; she still did not get up and open the gate.

5/16/93

I received information that some drugs were being picked up in visitation on Sunday and were being hidden around the auditorium area. Over to that area with several Supervisors search, never found anything. Lt walked up and was informed of what was going on. I was asked by the Lt. to go and deal with and unruly resident in Single Cell which at the time there was the assigned Sgt and two other Sgts. Already there after talking to this resident about 20 minutes and calming her down she complied with my request. I returned back to the control center. One of the Officers made the statement that was a BIG girl. I don't know what you would have done if she act a fool. So by her making the statement it lead me to believe, she was scared and I would not have been able to depend on her if I needed her.

5/18/93

The Lt. Had called EMS by request of medical. I ask Lt was anyone going to open the gate. Lt. to the gate, One Sgt went to relieve officer; I went to check out the equipment. The other Lt. stated the officer should be in the front of EMS. I told both LTs. in the pass the officer was to be with the inmate and have another officer to follow EMS out with the equipment. So guess who the chosen one was. I followed EMS Once we arrived I gave the officer her equipment. I returned to the unit and the Lt told me to go and assist with two other residents from Dorm D who was going to Dorm C to be searched and locked down. Returned to the office and the Lt. slapped me with the incident report to be done due to EMS being at the unit. Trying to obtain statements from all individuals involved. Medical questioning this, I told them to talk to the Lt. they stated they were going to talk to their boss. I told them they have to do what they got to do. I had talk to the officer assigned to that area and instructed her to obtain a statement from the resident. When I called the C/O back later and ask her about the statement she didn't have it due to medical staff. I let her no anytime a

Supervisor instructs you to do something; they need to follow through with it. Medical staff is not your supervisor waiting for the Lts. to come from in the back so we could go home. So I went to check on them and the Sgt that never do anything and scared of the residents was sitting with the Lts. telling something I'm sure. So then I get called back into the office. I was asked did I instruct the officer not to inventory resident's property. I told the Lt. I had not talked to that officer. I was told that I was responsible for that property. The other Lt. ask but who responsibility is it though. I told her it was mine, but I won't the only one here and you talk about being a team player. I stated to the Lt. that I would go to the warehouse and check for the resident's property and do the inventory to. The Lt stated no we are going home. So I grabbed up my belongings and headed out to go home. Once we were outside the other Lt. States to me it was your responsibility. That's when I went off, it seemed like they were trying to place blame on me. I stated Fuck this shit and I turned around and headed for the warehouse. I let the LT know I was going to the warehouse it was my responsibility. As I began to walk away the Lt stated we all are going to stay. The other Lt standing in the parking lot normally just gets in their car and leave, come up to me and ask if the property was located. I told her No!!! I got in my car and left.

MAY 21, 1993

I apologize to the Lt about the incident that occur the other night my actions and the statement I made. I was being treated unfairly and I became very upset. Lt stated she was going to get the Sgts in a meeting and find out what was going on, because there was a lot of tension.

6/11/93

Assigned to special housing. A resident was brought in from one of the counties and she had on a pink T-shirt and black panties and the smell of alcohol (assaultive) she did not give us any problems while processing her in. escort the resident to medical and I Was told that the resident would have to wait I inform medical No! she won't because she (assaultive) she was priority over everything else.

6/28/93

Assigned to Special housing in Single Cell to assist with an assaultive offender, who assaulted staff by pulling their hair and biting their finger. However, the offender began to complain about her hand. Sgt Ford along with another Sgt escorted the offender to be checked by medical. Called another Sgt to see if they could someone to pick up supplies, they are standing in the back talking to the Lt. and tells me to call control and see if there was an officer to do that. Why? Do you think I called your dumb ass! While in Single Cell handcuffs stuck on an offender. Lt. came to assist by breaking another key and using another key to get cuffs off. Relieved by 3rd shift and one Sgt that was conducting incident report ask for a statement on a earlier incident. Lt. told the Sgt we could leave and I asked the Lt. again was it o for us to leave and he stated yes, that Sgt was doing something. Another Sgt was at control on the type writer as I got ready to walk out the door, she states the count is not clear and officer replies yes it is. I told the Sgt goodnight I was finished with my work.

7/9/93

Assigned to Special Housing code 1000 called in auditorium in the office area where the offenders was backed into corner one had hand around neck trying to hold off another offender. They were told to let each other go as soon as the let go of one another Sgt Ford place handcuffs on the aggressor escorted offender out to medical and lockup. Myself and another Sgt was walking out to go home we heard another code 1000 called in Dorm F. Returned back in the unit to assist.

7/12/93

Out to hospital with an offender. While at the hospital the offender had a run in with a girl, looked like she had been in a fight. The offender stated that the girl was on crack and the girl heard her and came back. I ask the offender did she say something to her. I told the offender to be quiet and directed the girl to leave the area. The nurse directed the offender to go back in her room. The offender was going to be released but due to some trauma case coming in, no one could get to her. So now the offender starts raising Hell! Wanting to leave without signing release papers, I Sgt Ford placed my hand on the offender's waist chain to control her. Offender signed release papers and then tried to pull me as she was walking. I just put more restraint on that waist chain. The offender stated to me that she was going to get me. I kept it moving, and from only the vehicle never responding to her. The officers with me ask if I wanted her to sit in the back seat with the offender told her no! Returned to the facility and escorted offender to her cell. I was assigned to the Cardinal Unit when the manager received a call from the assistant Superintendent at the time who stated that two inmates were plotting to escape. The inmates were called to the office and both were escorted to lock up pending an investigation. Upon arriving to lock up there were no cells available, so then the asst supt custody an Ops had to have some inmates removed in order to lock up the two. All the inmates that were being released were brought to master control changed their clothing and was given their assigned housing. Then I had another inmate stating that an inmate had stolen her belongings and was on the grounds selling them. I went to Dorm F to address inmates about TV and after 5:00 pm the TV would be assigned channels majority rules TV to be turned, they would need to inform their Dorm Officer to turn the channel. I also notified the Officer of this before exiting.

I received my letter today about being assigned to the new unit (Falcon). Start Sept 7, 1993.

9-3-93

Out to the area hospital for reliefs and the nurse came to me just as I sit down in the chair and ask me was I eating in the hall. I stated "excuse me" I told her I had just arrived and she replied well I just asked.

9-5-93

Working visitation in the auditorium and officer find a small bag of marijuana and confiscated $6.00 from another inmate. This inmate was checked in prior to her visit beginning.

On Grounds for lock-in, down to the Phoenix Unit to wish the Sgt well. Today is her last day as Sgt going into management? Another Sgt calls on the radio looking for me. I told her I was en route to master control the Lt. wanted me. Lt. ask me where had I been. I told them I was on the grounds when they called lock in and had some offenders picking up paper off the grounds. Lt. asks was all the coolers off the grounds. I told them yes. Lt. stated it had been reported that the coolers from the din room are not being taken off the grounds. I then returned to admissions processing to assist with New Admissions. As I was being relieved one offender was threatening to undress in front of the control center.

8/16/93

I was assigned to B zone offender admission processing as a Safekeeper (someone being held for the county jail until they get sentenced or bonded out) Offender would need medical attention in which she would be house in that area. The offender was told that she would not be locked down provided she did well, and when she arrived she was locked down. Offender was very upset.

6/17/93

Assigned to special Housing I was sitting in the conference room and another Sgt calls me and ask was I through. I told them No! Why? The Sgt stated the offender that came in on yesterday has to go out to the hospital. I told her I would be there when I got through. To Master Control I was told by a Supervisor to let first shift know they will start the disciplinary. I left all information as I was instructed. Transported offender out to hospital hand was broken upline placed on hand /arm.

8/11/93

Assigned to special housing made rounds in dorm C on Safekeepers side. To the administration building for Permanent Status with the Assistant Superintendent, Superintendent Custody /OPS and Lieutenant. Received a 5% raised but only receive 2 1/2%. I learned the processed of accepting and releasing safekeepers.

8/23/93

Assigned in the Cardinal Unit offender had to be transported out to area hospital due to taking some type of unauthorized Drug. It was my understanding that the Drugs were being dropped on the yard on Mondays and the Yard workers are making the pickup. Sgt. Ford along with a couple of officers searched this offender room and confiscated 1 purple ballon with a white thin string attached in the hole of her room door. When I first made Sgt this Capt stated to me that I have to change I told her that was not going to happen, because I like me who I was now I may change the way I do some things. I was always reminded that I would not have any problems out of the inmates but it would be staff and this has held true through my career.

During this time the old Triangle facility was being closed down behind Central Prison. So there were 2 Male staff from there that came to our facility as Lieutenants. They have been the only males that stuck it through at women's prison, none of the rest of the males that came somehow did not work long. A lot of the staff that came to women's prison could not hang with the work load. If one of our people were hired at another facility they had been exposed to most of what then male facilities were just learning. When or if you ever work at women's prison, you had all the opportunities to learn, train and become knowledgeable. I made it my motto to work smart and not hard. I've always felt that moving up the ladder your work load should become much easier, less stressful but it turned out to be the opposite.

Phoenix Unit the newest unit was being classified as the old Dorm B1 and B2.

Another Unit was being built which would be called the Falcon Unit and I would be assigned to this Unit as one of the 5 Sgts. I was assigned to 1st shift which was 5:45 am - 2:00 pm 8 hrs then swing shift Sgt. This was a good time in my career because I learned so many things. I had pretty much grasp the respect of the population and most of the staff. We had our good days and bad. There was Unity though. Before we open the unit for the offenders we had a big old POT LUCK in dorm NB quad for our staff. I had cooked several items and brought including a big pot full of barbecue pig feet in which I really didn't know if anyone would like them or not. When I did go back to look in the pot, all I saw was knuckles rolling around. Obviously someone liked them. It didn't matter what holiday came I was always at that prison and short staffed. The Falcon Unit was uniformed Beds made military style, nothing hanging on beds, under the bed on the floor, nothing on top of the lockers. On the weekends Saturdays inspection offenders would have beds made lockers open and sitting on their beds quiet this was during count. If Items were found in these areas they would be collected and brought to the sgt office and when the inmates complain about their items missing they would have to claim them from the office with being counsel or being written up. Offenders were not allowed on the administration hallway unless they were called for or assigned to that area. My partner I worked with would have bad days and be in the office wrapped up in a blanket and the offenders would come down the hallway and peep through the window and leave saying I ain't going in there. When they saw her in that state, they didn't even bother her all day; because they knew it wouldn't be a good day. I had one officer she was always in the bathroom talking about she was cleansing her body. During that time we didn't know anything about toilet seat covers. So the officer would go in the restroom and line the toilet seat with toilet paper, before using the toilet. Well when they finish they never would take the paper of the seat. When another staff go in to use the bathroom this is what they were facing. So I have to talk to the officer and tell her "you are not the only staff that uses this restroom so before you come out remove the toilet paper off the seat. They stated to me, I need the toilet to be ready when I go in there. One day I had cooked Liver and onions for my dinner and they ask me what that was and I told them and they said I don't eat that. I said oh really. So I had some other staff to ask me to cook and bring some to work for them one day and I did. The staff that said they did not like liver and onions tasted it they about ate all the liver and onions up from everyone else. We had a good team working with us. We had our disagreements but we got over it and kept it moving because at the end of the day or night we all exit together. No one left behind.

This was also around the time when we were told that computers were going to be installed and all paperwork would be completed on the system. There were a lot of staff bucking the idea and did not like it either way it was happening. So you either got on board or jumped ship. It was a process, like anything else. Change is always good. It was a long process but we finally got the hang of it. It was a challenge to learn the system and the different things it could do. I was not a typer like others so it took me a minute. Over the years my pace picked up typing. We had to put reports UOF, Disciplinary in the system it was you pull up the screen and plug in the information and then type in some more information hit a button and the entire report would print up on a printer and it would be saved in the system that helped us do away with all that filing. Even though there were still somethings you had to do by hand.

Supervising staff is another book. Some of the staff that I have come in contact is so very disrespectful. During this period staff would switch days with each other to get a day off they requested the last minute and they both would sign an agreement stating this, but if one did not come in then the other one would have to come to work. Well this staff followed the process and one of them followed through with the agreement but the other did not. SO when they returned to work paperwork was issue. The one that did not show as agreed, was mad because of the paperwork and decide she would go to a higher authority than me. I have no idea what this Officer went and said but of course I got called, in trouble as usual. I told one of the superiors this officer didn't follow through with the agreement and she was receiving paperwork. Well obviously this was not was told. I was then questioned, if myself and this officer was having a relationship, I was completely knocked off my feet. I told them no! I was accused of having a relationship and I was not going back down to the dorm, I was being sent home. WOW! But the Officer was allowed to go back to the dorm.

I always got my first test whenever I moved into a new position. This particular time I was new to becoming a Sgt but could handle just about anything. So I had two very seasoned Officers that did not like each other at all, always bumping heads. When they had a run in with one another I called them in the office and allowed them to speak to each other in a respectful manner. WELL! That didn't work they start a verbal confrontation in my office. I then told them what I needed to say and informed them I will give you the respect because you are older than I am, but at the same time you will respect me and my position as sergeant and your supervisor. From that day forth I never had another problem with those two Officers.

One day I Sgt Ford was working this one offender I kept talking to all day and telling to settle down or she was going to segregation. Well about time to go home Dorm L Officer called me and said the inmate had gone in the quad where her girlfriend was housed. I proceeded down to the dorm and when I went in the quad inmate was standing at the bed with the other inmate. I gave her several directives to exit and she refused. When I pulled out my hand cuffs she left that quad and went to her assigned quad as I followed I passed the Officers desk took off my radio and sat it on the desk. Upon entering the quad the offender was upset. I told her she was going to lockup because I told her if she continued this was going to happen. Well the inmate was positioned between to bunk beds the wall and me. Yelling and being loud talking about she was not going, I told her Yeah! She was going her way or my way. Well she decided it would be her way. Offender then took off her shirt and bra. I told her it didn't matter she was still going to lock up. So then she put her foot on the bottom bunk bed and climbs on top and over to get away from me. I proceeded back to the rear of the quad to take control of her and she continued to refuse. I then got her in a hold and was exiting the quad with her and another staff showed up and she really started to not comply. I then picked her up from behind and began walking out with her and as I approached the door with her. The staff person positioned herself in front of us and I could feel myself falling so I let the inmate go and when I did that she fell on top of the staff by this time the desk officer had radioed for assistance and staff began to arrive. Once that offender was restrained she refused to get up and walk down the hallway. The offender was then moved down to the admin hallway with no clothing on. After which the inmate complied and was escorted to segregation. I remember one inmate in particular ask me was I ok, if I wasn't to let her know. LOL.

We would have inspections every weekend beds made military style quads in uniform style, lockers neat and clean nothing hanging on beds on top of lockers or under beds. This was our expectation.

We had reported for duty probably about 45 mins in to shift I was sitting at the desk drinking a cup of coffee when I heard code 100 code 100!!! I was like someone calling a code 1000 which would be a fight but was calling a code 100 which is ESCAPE! By accident, then I heard it again and it sound like the person was running, I pretty much jump across the desk wasting my coffee everywhere and exit my sgts door and I saw the back of the Officers heels running toward Dorm L side. I was like O SHIT! Someone is trying to escape. You know the worst part about it was that day we were fully staff. I had at least 8 officers in the Falcon unit. Other offenders were 10/ 4 for staff, and offenders got off the fence and pulled their hoods up on their heads so they would not be found out. Not possible offenders receive severe cuts due to the razor wire. The asst Supt was as having a doughnut sale and was at the gate house when they transmission came through on the radio. I then saw staff coming around perimeter on state and personal vehicles to assist. The Capt at that time closed the yard and conducted and institutional count.

I was sitting in the Sgts office in the Falcon Unit one morning and a inmates came busting in my office stating "now something has to be done about your staff, I told her to calm down and tell me what was going on. The inmate said your staff called me a Jigger Boo. I said what! What is a Jigger Boo, I didn't know what that was. So the staff entered behind her and stated I sure did. So I ask the inmate to step out and then I ask the staff what was a jigger boo, she told me but I don't remember. 1/7/17 I looked up the word and its definition. I then counseled with the staff and told them they could not be saying things like that.

One morning during daylight saving time some of the inmates would like to sneak behind the building in the canteen area after breakfast because it was still dark and have sexual relations, what we called a 23 sexual act disciplinary. So I went into the laundry room and heard all the sounds of sexual activity going on. So I told the inmates through the window when they were finished with what they were doing come to my office. When they entered my office they knew what was about to take place LOCK UP!

On another occasion in the Falcon Unit Dorm L Officer called code 1000 upon arriving in the quad offenders were fighting on bed that had no mattress. The offender was on top of the other offender with her feet hooked in the springs of the bed just beating the offender. I then began to remove offender from on top, when offender hollered out and said my feet. I was trying to get her off this inmate.

I was sitting in the office and an offender came to the door and requested to talk to me, while offender was sitting there explaining her situation and another inmate walked in and just interrupted and started talking and the next thing I know the inmate had jumped the other inmate. So I'm trying to get this chic off the other offender and somehow we ended up in the hall way, well my Officer stated he thought the offender was having a medical event. He didn't know offenders were fighting.

When I was coming through we had codes 1000 fight, 100 escapes, and 500 fires. Then code use the most was code 1000 fight. When a code 1000 was called you could see staff coming from all areas to assist and the inmates would be running behind you to see what was going on.

One thing I stop doing was wearing perfumes or oils with smells. This would attract the inmates to you. It was like bees on a honey comb. Inmates asking what perfume are you wearing. You smell so good. Some staff seem like they drown themselves with perfume or colognes before coming to work. However, some probably needed to. This caused inmates to hang around you and hold conversations and eventually you would get in an undue situation. Now perfumes, jewelry and etc are being smuggled in for payments.

We would go to the Business office and sometimes count out anywhere from $3000 to $5000 dollars to take on the compound to pay offenders. We actually walked through the compound with this money in our possession which was very dangerous. Each unit had a pay window and that's how inmates were paid every week. At that time the barter and trading was very significant inmate's money getting snatched, beat up and fighting. Back then we (sgts) use to have to pay inmates whatever they drew from their accounts before we became a cashless institution. One time they were only allowed to draw 30 or 35 a week and then it was raised to 40 a week. Inmates were only allowed have 5 dollar bills, one dollar bills and change, anything over $5.00s was contraband. Disciplinary action and monies placed in inmate welfare fund. The majority of the money was given in $5.00 bills and $1.00 bills and if you didn't distribute the funds correctly you would come up owing money out or not paying out the right amount. I would count it right there in front of them just like a bank teller and they are verifying that the amount is correct before they walk away from that window. It was always something going on never a boring minute. Most of the money paid to the population route right back through the canteen all that's not taken confiscated and place in the welfare fund. I was counting money one day in the business office I had like a stack of $5 dollar bills as I was counting I came across a $20 dollar bill I removed it an kept on counting. I think it was put in there just to see if I would turn it over. Once again I was being tried. Then the Sparrow Unit came along.

One day I was on my way home and I was leaving the Falcon Unit and I saw this offender sitting in the Sgt Office sitting in the chair with her legs folded Indian style. Once I got home I received a call to return back to the institution because there was an ESCAPE! What? I immediately returned and when I arrived I was informed who the inmate was and that when I stated this same offender was sitting in the sgts office when I left. Then we had Towers that were manned 24 hours a day excepted for enterprise tower where the sewing plant, diagnostics and the clothes house were located. Once the grounds closed at night about 9pm a formal count was conducted the count cleared enterprise gate is closed and the C/O would lock up the tower and come to master control. Once all the offenders returned to their bldg it was found that the inmate could not be accounted for. Later it was found that the inmate was hiding in the trash dumpster by the sewing plant once the count cleared and the C/O exited that post inmate hit the fence. Offender was gone 7 years before she was returned. During her time on the run she had a baby which was 7 years old another time we had 2 offenders to go over the fence by diagnostics I cannot remember that one though.

I was Sgt in the Unit there was this one offender she always cried wolf about having chest pains, but me along with another Sgt would always send her to medical to be checked. So this particular day I was not working the other Supervisor was there and I got a phone call from her stating that she had sent this offender to medical that day and she returned to the dorm. The offender was sent to medical again and she crossed over into Jordan right there on the floor. When something happens like that you try not to show emotion because you are not supposed to. I just could not believe what I was hearing it was unbelievable.

Hurricane FRAN 1996 was the worse Hurricane that I know in the state of North Carolina It was terrible I think I was at the prison 3 days. You needed to be where you was going because it came through here it looked like a war zone. We thought it was going to take out the fence by the Chapel. I was working at Michael's Steak and Seafood then. When we closed down that night the owners told me to take what was left to feed the employees and I fried chicken to take. We had no Idea it was going to be a ride like that. When the storm rolled in Falcon Manager myself and another person walked out the Falcon unit trying to get to master control Oh my God we like to got blown away, 3 hours later the eye came over and it was just as calm but when that back of the storm reached us it was terrible. Everything in Raleigh was shut down. I had staff that wait too late to leave home. They left home trying to come to work had to leave the first car flooded by water went back and got another car it flooded they were living somewhere near Crabtree creek. When they did get to work they were soaking wet from head to toe, I told them when they when home to get the second car I would have stayed home. There was no lights for a week had to revert back to old times heating water on the fire to wash off. Most of the roads were impassible due to falling trees BIG trees but you know them country boys they cut a path through and kept it rolling. Whenever a storm of that nature come through I always prepared to go to work early with extra clothing prepared to stay cause I always felt you go to the prison it was a safe haven. Three days inmates were locked down due to the storm they were fed in their dormitories. Once a fresh crew made it in then we would switch out while the others got a nap. If you did not know your way around in Raleigh you should stay home.

LIEUTENANT

When it was stated that tobacco was being taken away, it became scary, because smokers get upset, emotional, and mental that nicotine would had such a calming effect. When there were cigarettes the offenders were so nasty with it. It was a good job for offenders extra duty or volunteer work for the offenders that could not abide by the rules and regulations. I use to get about 10 or 15 offenders put them in a line give them a trash bag and they would pick up all the trash and cigarette butts. Offenders and some staff to would stand right there where a butt can was and throw the cigarette butt right on the ground. Tobacco products sold very well and made some good money I know. Once the smoking ended offenders began hiding, getting staff to bring in cigarettes for a lot of cash. One time we searched the canteen and found packs of cigarettes hidden in the glove box. If you just look at it you would just think it was a box of gloves, but that contraband was in there. Offenders would hide things in the most obvious places that you look at every day. Offenders would have cigarette lighters in their possession and the only way for them to get it would be through staff that was undue.

Visitation I was Lieutenant (OIC) on duty that day when I got a called from my Sgt stating that she saw a visitor pass something to an offender. I had the offender removed from the area and escorted the visitor out as we exit the gate house the visitor did a 2 step and he was gone (running) like his shoes were on fire. It caught me off guard this dude was 70 years old, by time I got my thoughts together this guy ran on me, he was down by the entrance gate. He was gone when the rover vehicle went to see if they could locate him. This dude was out of sight. My coworkers picked at me for days, saying Ford you let the old man out run you.

There was a code 500 was called in SCA upon me get to the area I was told that inmate was setting a fire in her cell. All the other inmates were removed and I gave the directive to the inmate to put down the matches several times and she continued to strike matches and put on clothes to catch. I got the fire extinguisher place the hose through the trap door and gave to long sprays. Offender came to the door put her hands in the trap which were handcuffed and the door was unsecured. When offender came out she had looked like a big old sun flower.

One day I was in a Use of Force in Mental Health and I was injured and really didn't know I was injured as bad as I was until the next day. I woke up and could not get my clothes on because my thumb on my left hand was swollen so big I could hardly move it. I went on to work and my supervisor instructed me to go to urgent care, in which I did and my thumb was severe sprang or out of place. All I know is when the Dr. put that brace on there I thought I was going to another city. LoL When I was Lt in Eagle housing we had this one inmate no one wanted to deal with because they say she was crazy, cause she was spreading feces all on the wall in her cell. So one day I went on the block and there was this horrendous smell, I was like what is that! When the staff told me what it was, I went to that individual's cell and I told her you are going to get all that shit off that wall. I had the staff to bring a mop bucket with hot water and mop and a scrub brush. I told them to open that door and the staff said you need me to go with you I told them no. The cell door was open and I pushed everything in that cell, I told that inmate I want you to wash these walls down and clean all that shit off that wall even down to the crevices. When I get back it better be done. So when I returned later that afternoon I went to that individuals cell and she told me Lt. I worked really hard trying to get all of it off the wall, but there is some that's still in the crevices that I couldn't get out. We ended up having to repaint the cell, but every time that inmate had to be locked up guess what cell she was housed in.

On duty one day and I had burned myself at my part-time job Micheals Steak and seafood. I had burned the inside of my arm when I opened up a steam box that had oysters. The Capt at the time ask me what happen to my arm. I told them and he stated you probably need to go to the doctor you look like you could have about 2nd or 3rd degree burns on that arm. Needless to say I still never went to the doctor. Using my own home remedies. However it did not leave me with a scar.

I was at the gatehouse viewing the camera when I observed an offender come in to visit and immediately the visitor passed off something to offender I watch her try to get it in her pants. I radioed staff in place already to remove her from visitation of course she acted as though what's wrong. I then ran from the gatehouse to the auditorium, as I ran other staff started running they had no idea what they were running for, but they knew if they saw me running something was going on. Upon arriving at the auditorium I entered the search area and inmate was talking staff was directing her what she needed to do, as I continued to watch inmate I observed her try to throw an object from behind her out of the area where she was being searched. I told the Staff there it is, that is what we looking for (Marijuana). The hands are quicker than the eyes.

When I was living in Johnson County I use to work at Micheal's Steak and Seafood on Cleveland school road where I met this young lady and she was a waitress. We use to hang out together at the oyster bar off of 42. We went kariokE and got plastered. So about 3am we both had to go home she went her way and I went mine. The worst decision I ever made. I was really high. I went on I40 going home, I was so scared the MAN! Was going to stop me, I said to myself it will be all over the news in the morning DOC employed arrested for DWI. Well while having this thought in my head, I saw blue lights flashing. I looked in my rear view mirror and there he was the MAN! Oh my God! I'm done I'm a cooked goose. But it was not me he was after it was another car that was behind me. I think I pretty much got myself together after that point. I arrived home on Jones sausage Rd. I made a promise to myself I would never ever do that again as long as I live.

I was Lt OIC it was a holiday as usual we were short staff and there were Managers and Capts and up assigned as duty officers then on the weekend. There had been something stirring in the pot for a while amongst population. This particular day it boiled over. The Sgt was on the yard when the offenders began to fight and the sgt called a code 1000 then now it's a code 4. When I went to the door and looked out all I could see were offenders by the main canteen as I made my way there and yelled move several times the offenders were not listening and would not move it was like they were in a trance. Upon me reaching the actual disturbance all I could see at that time was a uniform underneath and offenders kicking with steel toe booth. I had complete Tunnel vision at this point, trying to reach the uniform. I was told the next day that I was throwing offenders out the area. I called for any assist I shut down the grounds I pretty much came out of my uniform shirt. Once staff that could come out took control of the situation had offenders returning to their dorms. It was every bit of 500 offenders at that canteen they were waiting on the fight.

Christmas Holiday we would always try and have a Christmas dinner for the staff on shift, so this particular year another employee stated they would bring the turkey. So we were preparing and trying to get the food on the table and someone ask who cooked the turkey and when we ask why they stated the turkey neck liver and gizzard was still wrapped up inside the turkey. So that tells me that the turkey was not thawed and washed properly. We removed the turkey off the table. Unless you know people don't eat everybody's cooking.

One holiday Thanksgiving I cooked a meal for my unit to show my appreciation for the hard work they do. Even then there was staff that did not appreciate it. Some showed up so after seeing that they were only a few showing up, I let staff in other areas consume the food because I was not taking it back home. We always tried to do things to tried to keep that comradery going and fellowship.

Oh we are also an animal farm dogs, cats, snakes, birds, foxes, squirrels, hawks, geese, eagles. The inmates feed all these animals. The squirrels will practically walk up to you and ask for something to eat. LOL! I had an Officer that caught a snake on the grounds didn't won't to kill it, put it in a box and carried it to her car. When she got off worked that day and went to her car the box was there but the snake was not. It was in her car somewhere.

I was on the grounds during the night shift I saw a snake he was a good size, I sprayed it with my pepper spray that mother sucker jumped so high off the ground, I took off running. The birds would attack you at night try to fly at your head. I twist my ankle trying to get away from one.

We had an offender keeping a baby rabbit in her room in a bubble gum bucket. So I ask the offender before we searched do you have a rabbit and she said no. I then ask her did she have a rabbit and she said yes. I ask her what did she do with it and she told me another offender came a got the rabbit. I ask her who has the rabbit. She did not want to say because if it leaks out she told, the offenders will hate her. After going back and forth and searching offenders and they saying that the rabbit got away, no was rabbit found. I then went into the bathroom and searched and there was a bubble gum bucket sitting on the shelf with a flower pot on it, of course when I removed the bucket there was the rabbit.

I've pretty much been working part time since I started working at women's prison. I work at RDU airport exactly one week, I was supposed to be part time and they had me working 8-5 every day and I was working night shift. It was ok for a couple of days. Then we worked 8 hr. shifts. I was sleep I woke up I thought I had over slept heart racing I'm going to be late rush got ready for work went out got in the car about to pull off and I thought about it Damn I was off. I had over slept a couple of nights and my Capt ask me what was going on? I told her I was tired I was working part time. The Capt told me you need to be on time this is your primary job and it comes first, she told me if I was late again she was going to write me up. Oh my God I overslept the next night and she called me and woke me up Ford where are you, I said I'M on my way Capt I damn near ran out the house naked with my clothes cause I knew I was in trouble and was going to get some paperwork. I work Friday at RDU and never went back because I could not afford lose my JOB! Working night shift was a good shift for the most part there was not a lot going on maybe a few escorts and admin duties. You did have to put with some of the staff gossip, jealousy and staff all in your business. Most of the things that went on back in the day (old school) is happening now but at different levels with a new mind set of people.

One night we had reported for duty and we always had to make checks Tower 3 make sure the building were secure and the officer that made the checks that night came back and said they heard something in the Chapel. We went to investigate and you hear tell of people breaking out of prison not breaking into prison. I guess the guy was trying to stay warm so he climb the razor wire fence and broke into the chapel and blood was everywhere so of course we contact RPD.

Snow of 2000 I was off that day. The weather had forecast a large amount of snow. I continued to get up and go to the door looking for the snow and didn't see anything that resembled a snow flake. Well the weather man said it was snowing but it was not hitting the ground. I said Oh Lord they have made a forecast of this large amount of snow coming that they have miscalculated. Hell I went to bed later my dog woke me up to go outside to use bathroom. I open the door and tried to push the storm door and I could not get it open then I forced it open, Oh my goodness it was so much SNOW! and it was in drifts. I called in to the prison about 10 00am just to check to see if they needed me to come in because I Knew no staff could have shown up with all that snow on the ground. I called out to the prison and talked to the Capt (OIC) and they sounded like she was on her last leg. I told her I would come in and relieve her because I was not far from the prison but she would have to send a Rover to pick me up because I had a Mustang which could not travel in the snow. Capt told me well I will wait a few more minutes to see if anyone is coming. Capt called me back and said she was sending someone to get me. 15 mins the rover pulled up and transported me to the prison. The officer who picked me up walked to work that morning and he lived a long ways (that's old School). I arrived at the prison and relieved the Capt she was about to pass out. At this point I would remain until someone showed to relieve me. Which didn't matter because I stayed all night and the next day until thing cleared up along with the Capt she stayed also Management was starting to arrive and someone relieved me. Capt. and I were going to send out to get food to cook for staff because they had not eaten or didn't have money to get canteen. So we sent an Officer to the store he came back and it was absolutely nothing open. So we went to the dining area and grab up enough items to make a big pot of chili (These were emergency conditions) staff had to eat and that they did.

I was at work and I kept having these episodes of dizziness. The sgt told me to go to the infirmary and get my pressure checked, so when I finally did medical took my pressure and it was 200/120. The nurse told me I needed to go to the Dr. I told them I would be ok. So they called my Capt. they wanted me to leave and go to Dr. I told them I will go after shift was over. Then it was explained to me that this was a silent killer, I could have a stroke with no warning and I really would not want to be in a wheelchair for the rest of my life and someone feeding me or wiping drool from my face. However I did go and at that time I was placed on pressure medicine and been taking it ever since. I had a coworker who would always come in the OIC office on certain occasions and say to me Ford you ok. I said yeah, you sure your color has changed you look grey. I started laughing and they said no I'm serious. Well my coworker saw a change in me that I couldn't see in myself.

I was at work one day and I started having like muscle spasms in my chest. I came out the OIC office and went around by the holding cell, and it really started getting bad like a big ball and then it would relax, 30 seconds later it would go again. Well the sgts ask me what's wrong Lt Ford I told them I was ok while they were talking to me another spasm hit me, they ask was I having a heart attack. I told them no I think I was having muscle Spasms and they told me we gone call EMS. I told them you better not call EMS. If I was having a heart attack I probably would be dead by now. One of the sgt stated to me that's one of the signs denials needless to say I made it home and I called my Dr. the next day I was still hurting really bad.

I worked with a Capt everybody love them Big old teddy Bear. Their favorite saying when they approach you was "Hi You." When they retired we had a really big send off for them, topped off with a limousine ride to their home town. One of the Lts at the time drove for a limo company. We all pile in the back and just had a great time. When we arrived at their house, they said that's my motorcycle, I got to get it back on the road and one of the Lts said it looks like a motorcicle. We laugh so hard we couldn't catch our breath. They drove red Ford pickup truck. They were like 6' and somewhat heavy and to see them getting in and out that truck was hilarious. They look like they were stuffed in there like a sack of potatoes.

UNIT MANAGER

ICE storm this particular day I was a Unit Manager and that forecast again stated it would be a little light rain nothing significant. It started about 4p everybody trying to leave out go pick up kids and go to the grocery store before the shelves got emptied. I left going to pick up a child from school. I went down Bragg st and oh boy did I go down Bragg Street it was slick as a potato peeling. My truck tires literally bounced on the sidewalk to the bottom of that hill. I left work at 5p and I think everyone else did to. It was total kais all traffic was at a standstill in Raleigh there was no way you could go to get out of the lock up traffic when I arrived at home it was 11p that night. People were getting out leaving their vehicles and walking home, just left the vehicle in the street. It normally would take me 15 mins to get home not to today. There was a thin layer of ice that fell that day and accidents were everywhere. Kids were on the School bus all night. Dorm H was the dorm where all newly admitted inmates were housed and the numbers continued to grow. Sometimes you would have inmates that would come in and they would have LICE! Oh my goddness it would start pandemonium. We would have to send them to get treated for lice, all the clothing and linen had to be removed and replaced and most of the time it would end up being an entire quad of 34 inmates. Inmates don't like to be moved out their comfort zone, but when things start happen and become disruptful in the dorms you had to start playing musical chairs to keep down the confusion. I move an inmate out the dorm out the unit which they were housed in semi-private rooms to dormitory style. The inmate curse me out called me all kinds of different names in which I really paid her no attention. So then one day this same inmate still mad talking trash and cursing walked up on me while I was standing and monitoring the activities going on the yard. As I stood there smoking my cigarette the inmate got right in my face cursing and pointing her finger, I didn't flinch but I explained to her that she had about 3 seconds to step off me because I was not going to be held responsible for what came after. Other population inmates were standing there just watching to see what was going to happen. However the inmate did do as instructed, no other actions were necessary on my part. There was this one inmate she was scary to me when I started working at the prison, because whenever I would go do my rounds, she would be standing looking through the little window in her room door. You would hear water running I go and check it out and it was her. This inmate was the model inmate who had been incarcerated for a really long time and a disciplinary came across my desk where a staff had written her up. I was like WHAT!!! This individual had not had a write up since she was incarcerated. The write up was petty, however it did not get processed.

SEPTEMBER 11, 2001

A day the world will not ever forget WORLD TRADE CENTERS so many lives were lost that day. It makes my stomach quiver just thinking about it. It was like it was a dream. I was a work that day. All DOC was put on high alert.

To work in this type of environment was an adrenalin booster you never had a boring day/night because it was always something going on.

Bad weather days you bet not miss a day I called and explained to my Supervisor that I was going to try and make it I was told well I been here since 6:00pm and that's what I should have done came in early. I was told if I didn't come then I would have to talk to management. I stated that was not a problem I will talk to them and anybody else. The Supervisor repeatedly said I need you here. I told them I was trying to get there. If not I was going to turn around and go back home. Then the Supervisor told me to catch a cab. I told them my life was more important to me than any job.

So after that whenever bad weather was in the forecast I always prepared myself whether it was ran sleet or snow or Hurricane. Later on as I continue up the ladder as a supervisor, I could appreciate the lessons I learned. I continue the same tradition, someone had to be a work or come to work to relieve the already worn out staff that were there on post.

ER with inmate who involved in an altercation and was shoved through a window. Security at the area hospitals were always trying. Public was always looking at you and starring as if they may have seen a ghost, offenders would be treated differently and talked to in a negative way because they were incarcerated. As Security we would try to insure that the offender was treated appropriately, so that there would not be any problems, especially inmates with a behavioral problem. You would have medical to ask inmates what their crimes were which were not important, of course should not have determined the type of services that an inmate would receive but in most cases it did. We would have inmates that would hide items in their body cavity just to go to one of the area hospitals and the funny thing about it was when Xrays was complete the objects could be seen, but even medical could not extract the items. When we arrived back at the facility, the inmate would remove the item themselves and be like see what I got.

PERT 1991 when I applied to get on the team, I was told then that I had to have some military background. Well most of the staff that was put on then were not of military background and couldn't run from the gatehouse to master control LOL! I enjoyed being on the team when I finally got on there it was so exciting then. Our Supervisor motto was We looked good even though we didn't know what we were doing!

PERT had a two day outing at Umstead Park we had little huts we stayed in. Everybody was getting their belongings out of the vehicles and bringing them in when we looked up and one of the supervisors from our facility was coming across the yard with heels on and had a suit case with wheels we laughed so hard she was the first one that was put in the bull pen, which was a small area they would assign you to when you did something you want supposed to.

As you know everyone had been talking about snakes and them crawling in your sleeping bag while you were sleep. Well four of us were in each area so before we start putting our sleeping bags in a getting thing set up, we were checking the area and one person started running and we all ran. When we got outside in a safe distance we ask what are you running for and she said it's a big black snake lying up in one of the little cubie where we were supposed to put our clothes. One of the Officers said it ain't no snake in there and when he when and look he came out running to, it was so funny. Then another officer went in and came out and said it's a rubber snake. I was ready to hurt someone because we all could have injured ourselves. Well needless to say no one slept that night.

PERT was fun then we would go look for ANNIE a made stuffed human. Learned how to utilize a compass while we were in the woods looking for ANNIE we all would be in a line search that way nothing was missed. The next thing I know I was swallowed by a really big hole up to my head and I was hollering get me out, get me out cause I didn't know what was in there. They laughed at me for the rest of the night. Every time we go close to finding the Dummy they would move it making us stay in the woods longer. One Officer came face off with a deer she was yelling and screaming and the deer was just standing there trying to figure out which way to go.

Oh my goodness drilling ceremony we march so much I had blisters on both feet and bleeding oh our feet hurt us soooo bad, but we kept marching we stayed together and helped each other. We had a Ropes course-Morrison Youth this was a fun event but when we started the day the instructors had us to remove our head covers. That particular day the humidity was 100% and the temp was about 101. We were cautioned to continuously hydrate ourselves. Well we would have breaks and get water or Gatorade. After lunch we were preparing to climb the rock wall and do the Zip line. The instructor was directing us how to put on our harness and the instructor said to me are you ok. I said yes. He asks again and then one of my peers ask me the same thing. I told them I was ok as far as I know as I was standing there trying to get that harness on. 5 minutes Later the instructor told me to drop my harness I did and He had crank the Van and turned the air condition on full blast and told me to get in the van and stay in there and don't get out. He stated that I was dehydrated and he did not want to have to fly me out on the chopper to the hospital. I guess with him doing these exercises he was trained to see or know when someone was dehydrated. He stated he could tell because I was not sweating and my skin color changed. Needless to say I stay inside the Van while everyone else climb the rock wall and the Zip line.

Old Polk Youth Riot I was home in the bed I lived off Lake Wheeler road then, about 200 @ someone was beating on my door. I opened door and I was being told we gotta go PERT been activated it's a RIOT at Polk Youth center. With my adrenalin pumping I quickly got dressed and headed to Polk Youth Center that was located at the time off of Blue Ridge road near the Fairgrounds. I think this was on New Year's Eve. We were told later it all was started because a staff decided they would turn the TV off 5 mins before the ball dropped, that staff along with several other staff was injured. There was a lot of state property damaged. These are not good decisions making.

Drilling ceremony competition in which NCCIW won we couldn't win anything else because the men were winning everything. We pulled it out that year though and won it all and the trophy. We had different exercise that we would compete against each other and get points. So whatever team had the most points at the end of the exercise would receive a trophy.

We had Interstate Compact then where we would transfer inmates to other states to do their time. So PERT had go with the Federal Marshalls to assist with the transfer. I never had been on airplane in my life. Well guess what I was about to fly high in the sky. Just as scared as the offenders, but I could not show my fear. Some of the offenders carried on so bad they had to be put on the plane. The plane was so huge it was a Jumbo something with about 350 passengers US! I was told to pull my shade down so I couldn't see. I enjoyed the takeoff and it would take us 3 hours to get to Texas and you couldn't drink, after a while I let up the shade and look out the window and I said, I don't see no cars or nothing moving. Someone told me to shut up I couldn't see them because they was so small. Well we made it to Texas and when we landed Oh Boy! the Officers were out there with those tall cowboy hats on. Once we got the offenders off the plane we had to catch a plane back home we were given our plane tickets which was about 600.00 a piece and we were told if you lose it you want get on that plane without it. So we look up and here come a little short bus to pick up to go to the airport on the way the Capt look at his watch and said oh shit we gone miss our plane we late. That man driving that bus went so fast trying to get us there. If was about 12 of us we were running through the airport trying to get to the plane. When we arrive at our destination we were told no you not late you are a hour early, we all like to died we didn't realize the time difference. Well we came back and at the time there was a hurricane we actually flew over top of the hurricane. When we arrived back at RDU I kissed the ground and it was raining like cats and dogs due to the hurricane.

PERT was called out again to transport inmates to Rhode Island and of course I was one of the members chosen to fly on the plane. I had one of the PERT members to tell me Ford I will go. I said no you don't like riding the airplane (I show don't) but I was going to face my fears and go. So the night before oh my goodness it snowed. I had to travel from Smithfield where I was living at the time to Raleigh. I left home early that morning trying to get to the Prison and I could not make it I tried on 3 separate occasions. Finally I just called and told them I could not make it. Well that didn't go over to well with the Commander. I just did not feel safe out on that road from that distance. So once it became day light there were so many car accident, one in particular on I 40 overpass in Garner a SUV just like mine color and everything was hanging off the overpass. Several people and a couple PERT members call me thinking it was me in my vehicle. I told them no Mam! I'm at home I couldn't make that trip. So when I got back to work they was telling me that they had a scare on the plane which was a CROP plane all the alarms and whistles went off and it was because the plane was going too fast. Oh my God someone would have just had to shoot me and put me out my misery, that's all I would have needed.

Well about 2 months down the road I received a letter From PERT stating I was being removed from the team, after about 7 years. I was Furious! I couldn't think straight. I then went to talk with the administrator. I explained I understand why they removed me that was not a problem; it was how they went about it. Then I found out that another member was removed that was leaving PERT anyway. That was just a smoke screen. It was all good I got over it.

A few years later I was asked by the new administrator to become the Pert Commander for Women's Prison. I said let me think about it, I was a little reluctant and was not quite sure if I wanted to take on that responsibility again. After thinking it through and because of who they were I agreed. When I became the Commander for Women's prison Staff begin applying and requesting to know the requirements to join the "Elite." We brought on some very good staff.

One night PERT was called out and it was a very rainy night. So I had one of my officers came to me and said I just had my hair done and my eyelashes they are going to get wet. I told her you better take those damn eyelashes off and put them in your pocket.

Introduction to oleo Racism Pepper spray at hot topic LL. We all complained or questioned why we were being sprayed with pepper spray. The response to that question was if someone became disruptful or attacked you would know what the effects of pepper were and about how long it took to work. Well that was not a good enough response. So next the question was asked was well are you going to shoot me so that I will know the effects of a bullet. We were sprayed that day regardless of how we felt. A few people have to be carried to medical due to the effect. After it was all over with we all agreed it would work, so now were we going to be shot with a gun or hit with a riot baton to see what the effects was. It is quite effective. I've had them to take it in snort it up and hawk and spit right in your face.

I was escorting an inmate along with one of my staff one day to mental health when the inmate who stood about 6ft snorted and hawked up a wad of gunk out her throat, she turned to me on the left side and looked away then she turned to her right where my staff (male) and spit that gunk right on him. He was livid I instructed him noooo!! Stand by offender was put on the ground with her leg restraints and moved to master control.

Once pepper spray came out that would be our first line of defense and not have to become physical to bring down an offender. I have seen some suck that stuff right up and spit it back at you (Nasty). To spit on someone to me is the nastiest thing you can do or feces and urine.

One day I had arrive for work and I always go by the OIC to check in. This particular day the door was closed and usually I would peep through the little class in the door. Well both captains' 1st and 3rd shifts were in the office and one was standing by the door. The Capt. open the door, I said where the other Capt was and they stated he was in there at the desk. So me being who I am push the door open pass the Capt and started calling the other captain several times before they acknowledged me. As they turned around in the chair, I saw their face it looked as if they was having or had a stroke. I immediately call administration and advised them. Medical staff came over from the infirmary. Once medical arrival I was told to call 911. When I picked up the phone to dial 911 all the phones in master control were dead. I had to call out on the Back phone (old Phone) emergency personnel arrived and carried them to the hospital. Of course they said I'm ok.

I had two other offenders that were fighting right there at master control when I arrived I sprayed both inmates. After they were decontaminated, One of them stated I thought it was something coming out that thing (talking about air Compressor) burning me LOL.

Myself and one of my co- workers we always tried to do things to keep comradery going so one year we had a female basketball team. Which was very good I might add. So we would practice in the auditorium or just go and shoot hoops with some of the guys. So this particular night we playing a game one of my co workers came down on her foot wrong assuming she had twisted or sprained her ankle. They went to the get medical attention and found out the Tendon from her foot to her leg was severely sprained. When it happen she told me I thought you kicked me in the back of my foot, everyone was saying they heard it when it popped. Their foot has never been right since then. We were supposed to play in this so called basketball tournament at Polk Youth Center. Well needless to say when we arrived at Polk to play, there were like 21 women on one team and there was no other team. They had like 4 teams in one to our 6 players and we played and we won. No competition. After the game we stopped a Ruby Tuesdays and I fed everybody. They were very appreciative. Then we got together a coed softball team and it was so much fun. We did that for about 2 or three years until people kind a start falling off. I started playing with another team. We tried to have functions to have that comradery. Later on we began to have bake sales raise monies to have for staff retirements and feed staff to show appreciation for their hard work. For the most part staff appreciated it, but of course you know you were going to have those few people that would mumble and grumble. These same people never liked anything but were there to eat!!!! We had a few food functions for staff to show our appreciation and thanks for the hard work that they did. One time staff entered line up and was given a food check sheet to check what type of food they wanted. However they ask that's how it was served to them.

We had Towers 1 Gatehouse, T-2 behind dorm G which use to be dorm F, T-3 corner of E which is now F, T-4 remains same,T- 5 by vocational, T-6 is now tower 1 by SC, T-7 back by the fence behind wake advance. Dorm C was where the dining hall is now. At that time there was a little white building that was the OIC Capt Lts Sgt office. Sewing plant were all the inmate clothing was made diagnostics area. Which now are Tag and Duplication / Reg Maintenance.

At night the Supervisors were supposed to make a check on all the towers to make sure we were alert, but instead they would stand at the top of the hill and flash the flashlight and we were supposed to flash them back. So me being who I was wouldn't flash back so they would have to walk all the way out there and just as they started up the hill I would walk out the tower and they would be fussing saying why you didn't flash me back.

I had interview for a Capts position on several occasions, needless to say I was not chosen. Well all the Capts that were chosen before me was just passing through because none of them remained at women's prison I think it was a little too much for them. Then I had to train then how to do their job. One Capt was on the shift with me I was the Lieutenant so I would be very informative about how things were run. So I would be in the OIC office and they would always bring something for me to do, miscellaneous stuff. So I told them I was not their secretary. Some of that stuff they needed to do they need to complete it on the own. The holidays were coming up Thanksgiving and Christmas so I had requested to be off on Thanksgiving. The Capt and the other Lt. had requested to be off also after I turned in my paperwork. So the supervisor states one of you take off for Thanksgiving and the other take-off for Christmas. Well both the Capt. and Lt. Want both holidays off. That just want gone happen. So it was decided that I would do Thanksgiving and they would do Christmas. Well we had a little Thanksgiving lunch for staff. I was off but I had brought my food for the staff. Soon as I entered the visitation center, some of the other staff told me you know they called out. WHAT!!!! They called out. So I dropped my food and got the hell out of dodge because my supervisor would have made me work. So after all this had occurred. It seems that they were out to get me. I got to work one day my supervisor came into the OIC office along with the Capt stating they need to talk to me. I told them I was not going to talk to either one of you I don't have anything to say. I did not say anything but I got up to walk out the office and my supervisor tried to hold me in there, I went right on past her. Later on it was found out that the Capt had reported something's on me that were not true. Shortly after that the Capt went on medical leave never heard anything else about them.

I was Lt When a Sgt called a code 1000 in dorm H Sgt office all available staff took off by the way the staff sounded. Well there is a flower bed by dorm H and as I was running I came to the end of it and I knew then I won't going to make the jump because it was too high. When I did I jump I slid face first and I told the other staff to keep going, the officer who had really long legs step right over me. I got up and continued to the area. When I got there I found out this was an offender that was previously incarcerated and was released when she was on Max Con in Single Cell. When the offender came in as a New Admission no one checked her screens and she ended up being housed on reception. This was an assaultive offender. Upon me reaching the sgts area the inmate was sitting it the chair and she jumped up right in my face and starting cursing, just as I was about to address her someone grabbed me and said come on Lt. The next month I hurt so bad in my legs and hips I could just barely walk. I felt like my legs had been jammed into my hips, oh my it was so painful, but I continued to work. I did not go and have it checked out. I finally worked it out. You had to fill out a workers' comp and it was just so much, I did not want to do all that, so I stuck it out.

There were times a lot of them that I had to deal with that none compliant staff. I had an officer that I had instructed that she needed to write me a statement about an incident that took place while she was at the outside hospital. Of course she was upset because I requested the statement. When the officer came into the OIC office, I was sitting there and I ask them for the statement and they threw it across the desk at me. I then got up and moved a little closer to them and directed them to "GET OUT"!! When they exited the office I observed them, walking back and forth up and down the hall way, I then instructed them to go to their post and they fail to comply and while they were walking back and forth stated you black bitches and Niger. I was livid I again instructed them to go to their post and they started yelling. I told them you have lost your damn mind. Everybody come running out. So my Sgt who was always in the area somewhere pulled me by my arm and said come on Lt. and we walked outside. When I came back they were allowed to go home because they were upset. I was like REALLY! I'm upset to you gone let me go home. This human later on had me brought into the OIC office to apologize. I did not say anything and my supervisor at the time asks are you going to accept her apology. I still didn't say anything. I ask my supervisor was that all I proceeded to exit, I had nothing to say.

Somewhere during or after becoming a Lieutenant I thought I was going to become an alcoholic because I would go home and I felt I needed a drink to calm me down so eventually I could go to sleep. I started suffering with high blood pressure after I made Lt. terrible pressure headaches like migraines, not a good feeling. I think most of the staff that worked back then was taking some type of blood pressure medicine because things were becoming to be more stressful.

Unit Manager - Sparrow Unit we had a great team everything ran smooth for the most part we had different programs DART - Drug program Court recommended MATCH Mothers and their Children. In dorm O we housed the expectant mothers. When they came close to term they were moved to another housing area to be closer to medical unit. However some did not make it they would deliver on site at the medical unit or on the way to an area medical facility. I always wondered about so many women expecting being sentence. I remember reading somewhere that that when they go to court that the judge gave them a choice of whether to go do their time before or after they have their baby and of course they would rather go ahead and do their time so that the state could pay for their medical bills having their babies, I would to. I would say out of 100% of the expectant mothers about 50% of them would always return to prison on some little petty crime that would give them enough time to have their children on the state and be released shortly after that. There was at least 1 offender that had 12 or 13 kids in prison at the states expense.

In this Unit we housed Safekeepers inmates that were not sentenced awaiting trial and we would house them for the jails until they were ready to go to court. It was this one inmate they were very young, she always gave the other shifts problems during feeding times when they were being escorted to eat. Once they get to the dining hall this inmate would have to go to the bathroom. So I instructed my staff that this individual was not to utilize the bathroom in that area. So they would come back to the dorm raising cane. I would deal with them appropriately. I advised this person that they would take care of their bathroom issues before they go to the dining room. They would not go to the bathroom in that area anymore. If they had a medical issue she needed to fill out a sick call so that they could handle the problem. Later on when this individual went to court and received their time, she became attached to me for some reason. I always tried to treat them with dignity and respect. Most of the time they would listen to me, I listen to them, allowed them to come in my office and blow off their steam to keep them from doing things to get them in trouble. Most of the inmates appreciated that you were trying to do your job.

I had one Officer was just coming on and was having a lot of issues with the population inmates. I sit down and listen to them and was trying to get a handle on what was going on and the Officer stated I don't talk to them. I was like WHAT! That's your problem you are not communicating with the inmates. You have to communicate in order to your job. How you know what's going on in your area, what is happening with the inmate? After we had that conversation things began to improve. They soon became one of the most unlike Officers, but did their job.

I was the type of Manager I would take my radio home with me so when I arrived at work, I got out my vehicle and turn on my radio as I usually do. I heard and asst. Manager calling for the Lt. then followed by the Capt several times and then infirmary. It was just the sound of their voice letting me know that something was really wrong. I did not stop at the administration building that morning as I usually do I proceeded to the Falcon Unit as quickly as I could. Offender had crossed over into Jordan in her sleep during the night. So when offenders were given a directive to exit the quad this offender did not and she appear to be sleep after several attempts were made by calling her. After this occurred "rise time" was put into effect. All inmates were to be sitting up on their beds at 0600 for count. If they are sitting up we knew they were ok. Of course you had offenders complain about having to wake up at that time of the morning. It seemed like the offenders would be used to doing certain things doing the day. Staff should not have to wake you up every morning. Your body should be acclimated to waking up. We as Capts, Lts, Unit and assistant Unit Managers would report for duty in the mornings and stop at the Deputy Wardens office and I discuss different events and situations that had occurred or was going to occur that way we would all be on the same accord.

Unit Manager in Cardinal unit – It didn't matter what position I worked in or held at the time, there would always be staff that did not like you. I only did my job as require and beyond. Subordinates would go toe to toe, and tooth for tooth, knowing all the time they would be wrong, but I look at it as a test to keep me on my toes. One incident myself and a Sergeant were out out on the grounds and I notice the Lt sitting in the Bicentennial and the inmate look as if she was ranting and raving about something and me being who I am told the Sgt let go up here and see what's going on we have to look out for our male staff. As we approach the inmate was crying and emotional, so I asked what was going on and Lt. stated that something happen in the dining room with the Sgt that was supervising, as this inmate began to talk with me the Sgt came rushing out the dining room to where we were cursing that's what's wrong with these m…er f…ers now. You let them get away with everything. As I was instructing the inmate to go to master control, the Sgt became furious and acted as if he was going to run up on me. The Lt continued to try and calm them down. I ask them had they lost their mind, other staff then started to get me to go with them, I told them I was fine but they were not going to run up on me and do anything. All of this was going on out on the yard where all the inmates could see what was happening. I could her some inmates commenting at a distance. Meantime I continued into master control to talk with the inmate more and obtained her a food tray from the dining hall. It was not long after that I receive a call from Management about what happen and there were several inmates that were concerned about what they observed and how I was disrespected by the Sgt. And I needed to be seen on the grounds to let the inmates know I was ok. Of course as always I got reprimanded because of what staff stated that were there, but I didn't do anything. However, they eventually resigned. My supervisor had called me in several times about cursing. I admit I had slowed down a great deal. She stated to me that it was being reported that I was down there in the unit cursing. I told her NO that's not so. I felt like I knew the culprit that was alleging this. So I laid bait and the turtle bit it. So when my supervisor came to me again. I told them exactly what I did and who the staff was that were making the allegation. I told my supervisor well I can be just talking and get loud, first then the staff do is run and tell them or anybody I was cursing, to try and get me in trouble because they don't like me and they wanted me moved out the unit. Well that was not going to happen. This occurred often where I had to defend myself because staff was lying. My motto is I am here to do a job, not for no one to like me. I will do my job and you will do yours. It's not about I like you or you like me, because at the end of the day guess what? I am going home if the Lord says so. In this type of setting you trust no one everybody was your enemy. We always have a saying "don't bring your personal problems to work with you." That was really hard not to do. Whatever you do don't talk to the offenders about your personal life. This was how offenders would prey on you and make you a victim. Some offenders that's their MO. Offenders would see you were not having a good day looking down and depress, they would strike up a conversation with you and before you know it you have told them all about yourself and your problems in the outside world. Offenders saying how good you look sitting with you talking to you because you have some emotional issues going on at home then it continues with taking out or bringing something in for them. Once that happens they got you tied up and will use it against you over and over to control you. It didn't matter where you work male or female facility there was always dirty staff bringing in items for the offenders and the Officers been on the offender payroll. Staff getting involved in relationships with inmates I always said as well as some others why you want to come to a prison and have a relationship with someone incarcerated when you could walk right out the gate on to bragg street and get your groove on. Having dirty staff in a facility made it bad and dangerous for all of us even the staff that did their jobs. That was my biggest Pet Peeve I could not stand a dirty staff member. You are jeopardizing my safety as well as other staff "you got to go you got to leave." I would receive Information that contraband Syringes and pills were in a manhole by one of the units. Staff would bring in Marijuana and hide it in the flower pots flower beds for the offenders to pick up. Staff would come in loaded have the little tiny bottles of alcohol in their possession and are tore up the entire night offenders running the building. Usually when you do find out that staff is dirty it's when the offender has not received their goods or the staff double cross them just to get paid. Cigarettes were the hot commodity. Either staff smuggling them in or dropping them at a pickup point for the offender. $100.00 -$200.00 dollars a pack, singles for $5.00 and up I think. Most of the drops would occur in the mornings. Contraband is place in the trash or in the parking lot outside of the facility and when the offenders clean up the area they just make the pickup. There were so many Cigarettes found and some were right outside the gatehouse in which that was probably dirty staff. The drugs coming through the mailroom suboxane strips different colors that look like Listerine strips that you put in your mouth and they dissolve in your mouth. They would be on the stamps, under the flaps of the envelope, in a card from the kids that were colored with crayons. They have come up with every different way to get that drug. Well once the mail room got hip to it and looking at the mail much closer. They would move on and try to get it in another way. Dirty staff was the biggest of the problem because they would bring in large quantities of this stuff. They would be making a killing off these offenders because they would want this drug so bad. I was just so scared that we would find offenders overdosed on this stuff. The dirty staff bringing it in was getting high off of it to. During all of this you have staff to become emotionally and physically involved with the offenders. Don't put nothing pass staff because the very ones you think would not be working with the offenders just send you into a state of shock! There was this once staff that had some time in with the state and we knew they were bringing in items Cigarettes etc. but they were hard to catch. Finally they resigned due to the pressure put on them; the old saying is what you do in the dark will come to the light. The staff would come in with contraband tape to them strapped to them in their socks, shoes, bras, waist band however they could get it in and not be caught. I will have to stay one of the things we did not have to worry about was cellular phones being brought in. Maybe only 1 or 2 that I know of but we never found. Not like the male facilities. Most of the time you can get an idea, just by watching and listening which was a part of our jobs. Offenders would come with all kinds of problems and conversation about their families, especially their children. Some of the staff when they start working they are inquiring about what an offender's crime is. I would tell them that information is not required for you to do your job. The offenders have already been triad by Judge and Jury. Your purpose is the safety and Security and welfare of the offenders during their stay here. They are humans just like you the only difference is they have offender in the front of their name. They committed a crime and got caught so now they have to pay their time to society. Most of the times if you give the offender respect they will give it back. Some want you to make them abide by the rules and regulations because they don't know how. I've had several offenders to come and say they don't know how to make a bed because they have never done it before. There are so many young offenders doing time. They come in to the facility and they think they are on a high school campus yard. There is a big difference verses male and female like night and day.

When I was Unit Manager Dorm H a lot of work done to it especially the bathrooms and shower areas, after trying to get thing repaired and it never happen I started demolishing in the showers and that way they would have to be repaired. The material to repair them were on site it just hadn't been done. Several of the offenders assisted me with this. I had some offenders that love to stay busy. They love working for me. Even though some would work just to be with their girlfriend long as they done the work and did a good job, it was not a problem. They knew my expectations. I had several of the ladies assisting me with preparing for Accreditation. Offenders did most of the little things that facilities maintenance could not do, because of shortage of staff. They did tile and grout in the showers in all the units. The unit infirmary and mental health was transformed with painting, cleaning, replacing lights, removing old tile replacing it with new. Because it had been so long since any floor tile was ordered for these areas, we could not find the same tile. So the new tile the offenders made a design on the floor and you would never know the difference. Offenders much of them are so talented, some may have had jobs before being admitted as painters, or plumbers these ladies were so excited about their work and how staff and other offenders praised them and the work the done. The problem we always had was up keep. Women are not like men as far as floors. Some male facilities floors would be shining to the point you could eat off them. You come to women's prison though, it looks old but it was clean. Then there were offenders that were trained to do different types of work and they enjoyed doing it. They received training through the facility maintenance. However, that was ended. There were several that I could depend on to do different things, like unstopping water line or stopping leaks, having the knowledge of turning water off. One day I was called to one of the dormitories and I was told there was a leaks. When I reach the unit water was everywhere, I went down the hall to the restroom water spraying like Niagara Falls from the toilet a seal had burst. Long as you kept these ladies busy they were good. My Mom always told me an idle mind is the devils workshop. I had several ladies that accompany me downtown to the building DOP was in to repair holes in walls and repaint. So before we started the work I had a long talk with them and let them know my expectations and I would not give a second thought in preventing them from leaving the area, they understood me very well. So when the weekends came they were waiting for me to go to work. They enjoyed the fact that they got to leave out and enjoy the quiet. They did an excellent job on this project.

I tried to give offenders and incentive to keep their dormitories and bed areas clean by making it a competition. They like to compete against one another. Maybe request they get 1 merit day, be the first in line for the canteen for that day. Trying to go to the food side canteen Cardinal unit any day was a struggle. The main canteen had all the food items. The smaller canteens had less due to the canteens being so small. Inmates would fight because someone jumps them or someone holding a spot for them the line would just be soooooo long. Oh my goddness when you open the yard after the count, the inmates would run full speed ahead trying to get to the canteen first. Sometimes you would look up and you would see inmates in wheelchairs, walkers and canes moving very fast trying to get in line.

You want to talk about the hottest place in the summer the Cardinal unit made the name HOT! Miserably hot. We have fans but they were only circulating hot air. Offenders fussing and fighting over the fans, one room was getting more fan than the other. Then the bugs roaches and ants were trying to get air to. Women's prison is not closed in like most of the facilities through the state. Offenders wearing the little Bow Bow tennis shoes provided by the state that will only last about a week maybe 2. I've had offenders to come to me with holes in their shoes, bottom completely gone. Why? No one gave them more shoes. Offenders at women's prison are just exposed to the outside elements trying to get to various areas of the institution. When it rained you got muddy there really are no run off for this unit and the water would be rushing down the hill like a river there were some staff that would actually take off their shoes and walk barefoot, when cold weather started you were cold, When it snow you had to be out shoveling snow deicing the walkways for staff and offenders to travel on safely.

The Gate house was very poorly designed as for rainy days. This place would flood, water up over your ankle and you would have to walk through this in order to get to your destination. In the gatehouse you had all this electrical equipment, carpeting on the floor it would stink and mildew, it was terrible. You would have staff with squeegees trying to push the water out but it didn't work because it came in so fast along with all the mud, there would be visitors standing outside waiting to come in to visit with inmates, they would be soaking wet. Now it's worst because no one is allowed to bring umbrellas on to the grounds. Since I retired I think now there has been a canopy placed from the rear entrance door of the administration building to the end of the walk way.

CAPTAIN

As an OIC you would receive so many crazy calls from the public and one of the things that stand out in my head is the public saying we are supposed to rehabilitate the inmates. What they don't understand is we don't rehabilitate them; we provide them with the tools to rehabilitate themselves and try to get back on the right track before going back out into to society. Most don't make it and end up back in prison, sad but true. Society will not give them chances to make themselves better and be able to provide for themselves and their families.

One night I was called back to the prison, Institutional count was conducted and the count was coming up short one offender. Once I arrived at the prison I was brief about what happen. When I started thinking about it and putting the information together in my head. I said whoever it is they are still on the compound they are hiding. I then proceeded to the area and I heard some traffic over the radio about the green house area on the yard. Well myself along with another old school individual went over on the compound and went down to the area of the greenhouse and we looked in placed no one else would think to look. Staff also was in the area searching and had searched inside the greenhouse several times and came up empty handed. Well then I was talking to one of the facility maintenance workers and they stated they saw someone standing between the greenhouse and the canteen. By this time staff had exit the greenhouse and one of the sgts heard something. So they opened the greenhouse back up and when back in and that's where the offender was. The offender was so small she probably could have hide in a trash can and you would not know unless you actually looked in there. The offender was under the table behind some flowers and if the sgts had not have been persistent, who knows what could have happen. Our institutional counts were terrible either they were counting too many not counting enough or not counting at all. I had tried to explain for a while the generation of Fowlkes we had did not know how to count in their heads or on paper to add numbers, because when they were in school they were brought up using calculators that add numbers for them. So if they didn't have a calculator or someone in that area to count, it was going to be a bad day. It was a bad day almost every day. I would always know that someone had miscounted. I had explained to management if someone was gone I would feel it, I didn't have that Erie feeling.

We conducted count one day and we were waiting on a facility to call in their count. I told someone to call and see what the holdup was. Meantime I received a call from police dispatch that there was a Lady at the bus stop stating she was from women prison they gave me the name and come to find out this inmate was from the facility that we were waiting for the count. I immediately got some staff on the road. I ask them to hold her there we were on the way. If we had not have receive that call, it would have really been late finding out from that facility that an inmate had actually left. So it was always important for you to know the location of all inmates in your custody all the time. This Unit was a minimum custody unit it's security was not the best because the main entrance door you had to buzz to get in, but you could walk out that same door and not be detected right into the public and no one would know until count or offender told it. We were very lucky that day that that offender called, they probably got scared. However since then changes have been made where you will have to buzz to get in or out. Its funny how you can talk and make your concerns known and no one listens or reacts until something major occurs and then things are changed.

I got a call at home one night that the Falcon unit had caught on fire. My first thought was the offenders have tried to burn down the unit. However a boiler had caught fire in the boiler room. Raleigh Fire department was called.

I was called one day to go to Fountain Correctional because an offender had escaped. Offender escaped from the dining room that morning. It really didn't take a lot of effort to leave. This was a minimum custody facility. The offender was located that day and returned eventually to Bragg Street Women's prison.

One day I was in Control and I heard a radio call for all available staff at the tag and duplication plant. Everybody took off running. Be advised there were about 20 steps to run up cross over the bridge and come down 20 more steps. Your adrenaline pumping and once you reach the area they tell you it is a disaster drill what?!!!! I'm dying slowly trying to get air in my lungs along with a few other staff. J

Another time I was down the hill near the small canteen and a code 500 fire was called in the auditorium. There I go running again, in my mind I'm thinking if this building is on fire it's going to burn to the ground because it so old. Arrive at the location several officers came running with a fire extinguisher; however this was a drill, to see how fast staff would respond. I'm standing there trying to give them lungs some airJ.

Don't let a disturbance happen out on the yard or in a dorm all the way down the hill. You start running the offenders start running to, all in the way you telling them to get out the way so you can get through. The worst place on that compound for a disturbance was in the dining room. In the old dining room (Chicken Day) all the staff hated these days. Inmates that never ate came to eat on those days and the really smart ones would it twice. The line would be so long it seem like you would never get out of there. Inmates breaking line it was terrible and adrenalin pumper all at the same time, but we did it. Then when the inmates got into a fight if you were across the dining hall inmates get into a fight you have to get there by the quickest means, A couple of times I have gone across the table stepping in inmates food trays and all trying to break up a fight in that dining room. Inmates would be like you stepped in my food. I would tell them don't worry, I would go and get them another tray of food to eat and they were fine. The new dining room was built which was a lot better. When the offenders assigned to prepare the meals get in a brawl. There are so many weapons that could be used. So that's kind of scary. Most of the utensils are kept behind a lock and key for the most part. Offenders are supervised when utilizing them, Offenders would always bring out food of some type and carry it to the dorms Onions, chicken, cake etc: you name it. Offenders were pat frisk most of the time before leaving the dining hall. There were a few that got through hiding items in their underwear, socks, bras, under shirt. They were getting the items so at night when they are sitting and watching TV with their girl or other offenders they would make what they call dinner, with oodles of noodles, chez curls etc. offenders would have birthday parties for other offenders and make a whole cake w/ icing out of the items they purchase from the canteens. Don't let a utensil get missing from the dining hall, no one is allowed to leave the dining room or the institution until it is found. Most of the time is would be in the trash that was in the dumpster. So guess what? Offenders had to go dumpster diving! Yes in all that food and trash that had been thrown in there previously. Usually that's where they would find it. Dining room inmates would deliver food trays to segregation dorms (Eagle Housing Unit) that how contraband would get into those areas. Offenders would leave letters and notes etc: in the trays for the other offenders to receive. I told them one day the food carts need to be put on a conveyor belt every time you turn around, one of the workers was always getting injured hit w/cart or run over. Then of course you have to do all this paperwork, offender accident form and incident report. There were so many accident incident reports coming from the dining room. When an inmate didn't want to work for a couple of days that was the way to go, get an injury or go to the dorm slam your hand in the locker or the door.

Working in the dining hall there had to be staff assigned 1 supervisor normally a sgt and 2 or 3 officers. Once the offender scanners were put in there had to be at least 4 officers and a Sgt. 2 C/os scanning and the other two monitoring all those inmates in the dining hall and the offenders still found a way to eat 2&3 times, officers from the 4 units Phoenix, Falcon, Sparrow, Cardinal, Operations. It was very seldom this happen. Then when you had staff in there they would not do anything but stand around in groups and talk, not monitoring the offenders. Most of the time we were short staff so we made do with what we had. A lot of staff couldn't stand to go to the dining room to supervise. That was one of the worse places to be if a disturbance broke out at any given time you could be supervising 300 + offenders in the small area. Offenders want to sit by their girl or their friend or I don't want to sit by a certain person. There was a seating order that the offenders would have to sit as they came out of the food line they were to fill each row in order. So a lot of times what they would do would hang around at the drinks section and wait on their friend so they could sit together or carry each other's tray. When staff saw this occurring it would be stopped and most offenders say well, I'm not eating because they can't sit with their friends. This has been done since I began my career there. It's done because there are over 1500 offenders eating in the one small dining area. So offenders in and once sitting had about 20 minutes to eat and they would rotate out and the next group would come in to be fed. We often tried to feed by units because it was so controlled and that the way it was done when it first started restricting the grounds. The units would rotate every week of who would be first to eat. This would continue until all the offenders were fed. This was put in place years ago when the Capt. wrote the policy that the grounds would be restricted and the Sgt and the officers from the area would escort their unit to the dining room to eat and back to the dormitory. This was done breakfast, lunch and dinner. Some supervisors had supervised the dining hall for so long they were masters at it? They would roll those offenders in and out of there in no time. I believe sometimes they did it to compete against one another to see who could complete feeding the quickest. After a while with new staff coming on board, things would go array and when you try to put it back in place there were problems. I would try to always try and make things easier and more controlled and of course when I did this there were supervisors that did not appreciate it. So then I was called in by my supervisor because the supervisors had complained about going to the dining room with their units. At that point I was done. So what I began doing was controlling the offenders myself with the yard officers. I would get my Speaker phone and go on the yard and have the offenders to return to their housing areas. This was done at lunch and dinner. Well one day I received a letter and I was referred to as a 'Porch Monkey'J me being called out my name was hilarious. We always would have some type of food selling through the women's club. Inmates were able to order outside food items Chinese, pizza, Smithfield. Pizza was the hot item though they love it. One week they had sold Chinese food and the inmate was standing outside with the food in her hand and another inmate just walked by and snatched it and took off.

We always had a 4th July celebration for the offenders they would have different competitions going on units competing against each other. Lunch served outside hamburgers and hot dogs cooked on the grills. The offenders really enjoyed that. Programs would have talent shows and plays these things kept their minds occupied for the most part, they were excited. The plays mostly were written by an offender, so much talent. There would also be dorm judging at Christmas. Where the judges would be from other agencies and they would come in and judge the dormitories for their decorations.

Bake sales and cooking on the grills to raise moneys. It would be such a harmonious time and we looked forwarded to it. Myself along with another staff did the cooking on the grill and everyone pitched in and brought items and the food was good to. We enjoyed ourselves we enjoyed these times sitting, talking and listen these times are when you found out information you had no idea. I love to cook and I love to watch people eat and enjoy themselves eating.

One Thanksgiving all the supervisors pitched in and brought food to feed the staff. We had some of everything I had grill 5 turkeys on the grill. I had to work that day. My Mom and I had already prepare Thanksgiving for home and I knew she would be ok, because all her favorite men were coming her 2 sons and wives and them 2 grand boys and the great grand ones.

Single Cell A I was assigned as one of the Unit Managers I exited from back in the office area when I heard a lot of tussling around and loud talking, when I looked around the corner to see what was going on staff was pinned up against the wall by an inmate. I entered the Block placed a firm grip on the offenders restraints gave her a tug and told her to come on and go to her cell and she complied.

As the Capt and the shift Commander there was always something going on? I heard a call over the radio for medical assistance at one of the inmate work assignments, I called to see what was going on, I was informed that inmate had broken her foot and the staff stated to me I know its broken. At this time I proceeded to the area and when I saw the inmate she had slipped and fallen on the floor, her foot was completely turned the opposite direction, dislocated and broken, but she did not seem to be in any pain.

One time I came in for duty and shift reported that they had been doing searches in different areas trying to locate a sex toy (DONG) that the offenders had made from some of the materials that they use to make denturon. They wo ir so creative who would've thunk it. They had created a dong Large, Medium and small and it had the veins and all as it was explained. Well staff would search after getting a tip and would be told by the offenders ya'll move to slow, it's been moved. So this homemade toy was being moved around from place to place. As staff gets closer to finding where it was it was ditch in a common place so no one would get blame or receive a write up. Once it was locate and turn into the Capt, they was like how does it work "LOL" so one of the other supervisors put that thing on, it had a harness and all that LMAO. It was making its way through those units offenders didn't want to give up a good thing "LOL". Inmates would make hooch something that damn near would kill you. We would find containers with fruits and yeast sitting in a common place fermenting, so they could make alcohol especially around the holidays.

Correctional Officers who were expecting when I started my career children are old enough now and working. That just feels kind of weird. I don't know who they are unless they tell me.

I have met some interesting people along the way in my career. Some I learned from laughed, cried and enjoyed just being in their presence.

A lot of the younger offenders think they are at a college campus with their friends. You have the older offenders that may take some of the younger ones under their wing and help them to understand the way of prison life. They will have their little families Mama, daddy, brother, sister, grandma, granddaddy. You also have offenders that become involved in relationships. A lot of the women coming in would have this saying I'm strickly D…ly that was a laugh, along with most of the staff. Some that has never been with a woman before and they just totally lose they mind. Most women that come into prison have never been with another woman before. So when they have this woman that is being good to them and taking care of them buying them food and spending time with them, they become so involved and curious of what it's like, so they get caught up. Most of the time these offenders get involved they have a disagreement or trying to break it off, It ends in a lot of disruption fighting and arguing. Well of course this causing disruption on the yard and in the dormitory. Correctional staff then steps in to try and settle the problem which ultimately ends with lock up. I express to the offender you are here to do your time and go home. When you came here you chose to get involved in a relationship, that's not a part of your treatment plan or your sentence. You get involved in a relationship and now you come to Staff to help you get out of it. I use to tell the offenders when you step in front of that judge you were by yourself. No one can do your time for you. When you leave prison you will leave by yourself. When I first started working at women's prison it was shameful to you and your family to go to prison. Most families would disown you. Now it's not a big thing. Most of the public seems to think we rehabilitate the offender. What the Public don't understand is that we don't rehabilitate them; they rehabilitate themselves with the different programs offered to them.

Most of the inmates are very talented and resourceful. You wonder why are they are in Prison many committed a crime and others took the fall for someone else that committed the crime. They use their hands and minds so well. Where we the public go out and buy what we need or want they make what they need or want. Drawings, Crafted items it will amaze you the talent that they have. Once they are released back into society they have a very small chance of being hired for employment because of their crime. Some employers are not willing to take a chance in hire them in fear that it will cause problems in the business world, with that being said they will revert back to the life of crime, drugs and living on the streets to survive eventually back into the system where they know they will be taken care of at the expense of the tax payers or dead.

My rotation could never get the count right, but I always knew that no one was actually gone they just couldn't count or do a paper count or put all the numbers on the paper and not be able to add or take away a number it was terrible. This happen every day, sometimes we would be in count for hours to figure out where 1 inmate was or 20 inmates were. They were there the staff either couldn't count or add. During these times I always knew for some reason that no one had gone just by my gut feeling. One night we had a count way over until the next morning about 2:00 am. So my fan club had stated that I did it intentionally to teach them a lesson which was not true. I had to return back to work that next working just like them. Why would I deprive myself of much needed rest? We later found the problem which should have been caught earlier in the game. Lord, Lord, Lord the next day I was summoned to administration. When I was questioned about the count incident and was told what the staff alleged it just made me so furious. I was about to be sitting on the couch. That was the little spot for any and every one that got in trouble. No one likes the couch, although some did because they did not have to work and was getting paid. The couch has seen a lot of different pant seats. LOL!!! Sometimes I would just go over there and sit just to see who would come by and see me and go back almost tripping over their own feet to tell someone. Word travels warp speed at that place.

Being a Department of Correction employee is so very demanding; I'm talking about the women and men that are on the front line that has come up in the department. We as a correctional staff are so abused mentally and physically. You are told everyday this is a part of the job don't bring your personal issues to work with you, but that is very hard not to if you have something going on at home with your family it is very hard not to. When you report for duty it all depends on what is going on with you, dictate what that tone for the day will be. We as Correctional employees don't get enough credit for the jobs that we do every day keeping the general public safe. We continually are mentally abused by the public first calling us "Guards." that should be corrected because I get really angry when I'm called a Guard. There were guards back in the day this is the future. When I put that uniform on every day I had respect for it and everyone should have the same respect as well as all law enforcement officers. There are some that are not worthy of wearing it to hide behind to carry on criminal acts. There are people that sit at the round table every day and discuss corrections but has never been in a prison and don't know how it's operated or by who and how many. They go by their statistical reports and numbers. You can write anything on paper and make it work. Correctional staff are face with from a 1000 to 1500 inmates to maybe 70 staff each shift which is not enough staff but we are there for safety and security of the offenders as well as the public. It takes a well-rounded individual to go through the adventures of Prison. You as a correctional employee have to have morals, be respectful, and perform your job duties in a respectful way. Working in a prison environment and being at that same prison your entire career, you bond with other staff and you began to form a since of family. The One thing I would like to see happen is that NC Correction for Women receive the same pay as Central Prison who receives 10% more because there facility is headed by a Warden / Death row. NC Corrections for Women has had Warden status for some time now and always had death row population, NCCIW should be allowed to receive the 10% as well. NC Corrections for Women is only female Maximum Security facility in the state of NC. We don't have the pleasure of moving inmates from facility to facility because they are hard to manage, assaultive, predators, active gang members. We had to deal with all of that and then some more.

One of these people that sit around that round table that I was talking about, came up with a training that they were going to get all staff trained how to talk with the offender before having to become physical. WELL Surprised!!! Y'all we been conducting business like that since I been working at Women's prison. They may need to teach it to the male prison staff. So this does not come to women's prison as a shock.

I saw a lot of staff get promotions some good some not so good. As a Sgt you were that in between supervisor you had to learn it all plus administrative duties. When I was coming along at that time it was a challenge to me and my peers and we enjoyed what we did. It has changed now because they don't want to put in the time and work just skate by until they can make it to the next level of promotion. So now you have a bunch of Officers wearing stripes and bars and in management that are not willing or had spunk to get out there and do what the positions are required for them to do. The old saying you can lead a horse to water but you cannot make him drink it. I would say out of a 100% of the staff that supervise now 35 or 40% of them do their job to the best of their ability, the others are dead weight that others have to carry around. In this business you have to start with respect of yourself, be a leader and not a follower. Be able to make a decision and stand firm by it. If you are wrong own it and keep it moving. People that lie, steal and cheat don't get very far.

There are and always will be the new Correctional Staff but the one thing I request of an individual that has never been in a prison setting before is to use their five senses hear (LISTEN),What's going on around you at all times (LOOK)see, (FEEL) no emotions, personal (TOUCH) No One (SPEAK) only when it is absolutely necessary. Being a Correctional employee is a common sense job. Common sense is not teachable it's a part of life and growing and maturing. Some think because they went to a big college that they are better than others. Sure you will come against situations that need to be weighed out; other situations come natural because they are common sense approach. You come into prison with a low self-esteem several staff and the inmates will pick up on that. Don't get involved with your peers or inmates it will only cause you problems down the road. Don't ever think what you do will stay in the dark, trust me it will always come to light. Be proud of who you are and that uniform you wear be respectful and you will be respected. Some staff comes in line up tore up from the floor up. Smelly, muddy shoes, uniform all wrinkled, no name tags, just a hot mess. You should come in Sharpe uniform wrinkle free; shoes shined or not dirty with all your gear ready to take on your assigned post wherever you are assigned to. From the time you leave that line up room you are the one that will set the tone of how your day will turn out. Don't sleep where you work it always causes drama my mom told me that many moons ago? You have to love what you do. I lost My last 2 years were my worse to years at the prison. There were times I did not want to go to work. I dreaded getting out of my bed in the morning at 3:45 to go to a place where I would not be appreciated by some and hated by most because a did my job. I knew when I starting feeling like I was I knew it was time for me to get out. Administration had been change once again. It was all about how it was done that really disturbed me. The first Male Warden of my career replaced the previous -Warden.

Staff stating I had threaten them in line up, which was not true. I was the supervisor that you would not turn my line up into a showboat. I would make the staff leave out. I would allow them to voice their concerns in line up pertaining to the job. Personal concerns they would need to talk to me privately because line up was not the place to discuss personal issues. However, they would complain and I would ultimately be the one who was moved because I did my job, which I was very upset with just reason. The staff was dirty and knew they were dirty and that was just a ploy to get me out the way so they could bring in contraband. Staff came in one morning and they were targeted for a search, this one staff assumed I had targeted them and I had no idea that this was going down myself. In which they completely refused and were just totally rude and disrespectful. Later that morning they were still allowed to enter the institution without being searched. This all was under the new administration put in place. The new Deputy "Little bully" Warden carried on a grudge against me for years, I had no idea. This was because I was chosen as lieutenant many years ago over them. How does a person carry something around with them like that for so many years? So now this person begins harassing me about little things. One of which was going to the corner to smoke. They told me I could not do that, but other staff was allowed to because they work 8-5 and they had a lunch break. I was told I work 12.25 I said NO I'm here longer and later than any of my staff more like 13.50. So then I was informed you have to utilize comp time to smoke I stated not a problem. So the next few days I was called back to their office and they had pulled all, I mean all my 113's. These 113's don't show where you took comp time. I told them it only takes 5 minutes to smoke a cigarette at the same time I still handled my business. So they say to me I'm not the previous Warden. I was just too done. Scared they would miss their accolades "Big Dummy." Once I mentioned I was going to retire. They stated to me go ahead and retire. I said to myself this person will use other people to make themselves look good for the higher ups. I can only talk about the few minutes I was there under that crazy administration. I had to get out because I could not lose 28 years because the now deputy warden has been holding a grudge since I made Lt somewhere around 2000 and still carrying it. I had already checked on my retirement 2014 after my mother passed because she told me it was time for me to come on out and let someone else have it. Most of the time if you don't follow what your Mom tells you something will happen and it did with me the new fowlkes. Well I could have retired in August 2015 my papers were ready. I said to myself no I'm going to stay till my year 2017. Then I began being harassed by the "Little Bully" that was it for me. December 1, 2015 I submitted my paperwork and December 31, 2015 I walked out that gate never to return. It felt like the weight of the world had lifted. I had to keep telling myself that I was retired. Whenever you get to the point that you dread getting out of your bed going to your job it's time for a change. Life after retirement is GREAT!! Although I miss my people and communicating with the inmates, I still talk and keep up with most of the staff sharing old war stories and catching up on the new ones. Working in this type of environment is very dangerous, it is so unpredictable. One minute things are quiet and ok and the next minute all hell breaks loose. So many things can happen from being injured to losing your life. I employ all staff in Department of Public Safety to always be aware of your surroundings. Watch for those RED flags. Most of the employees in Law Enforcement are over worked and under paid, but we still take that risk of dealing with out of control individuals every day to help keep the public safe.

Milton Keynes UK
Ingram Content Group UK Ltd.
UKHW012133131223
434271UK00003B/46

9 798890 317865